Agency Operations and Sales Management—Principles of Agency Management

Agency Operations and Sales Management—Principles of Agency Management

Edited by

Mary Ann Cook, MBA, CPCU, ARM, AU, AAI

4th Edition • 2nd Printing

The Institutes
720 Providence Road, Suite 100
Malvern, Pennsylvania 19355-3433

4th Edition • 2nd Printing • November 2015

Library of Congress Control Number: 2011945300

ISBN 978-0-89463-528-1

Foreword

The Institutes are the trusted leader in delivering proven knowledge solutions that drive powerful business results for the risk management and property-casualty insurance industry. For more than 100 years, The Institutes have been meeting the industry's changing professional development needs with customer-driven products and services.

In conjunction with industry experts and members of the academic community, our Knowledge Resources Department develops our course and program content, including Institutes study materials. Practical and technical knowledge gained from Institutes courses enhances qualifications, improves performance, and contributes to professional growth—all of which drive results.

The Institutes' proven knowledge helps individuals and organizations achieve powerful results with a variety of flexible, customer-focused options:

Recognized Credentials—The Institutes offer an unmatched range of widely recognized and industry-respected specialty credentials. The Institutes' Chartered Property Casualty Underwriter (CPCU®) professional designation is designed to provide a broad understanding of the property-casualty insurance industry. Depending on professional needs, CPCU students may select either a commercial insurance focus or a personal risk management and insurance focus and may choose from a variety of electives.

In addition, The Institutes offer certificate or designation programs in a variety of disciplines, including these:

- Claims
- Commercial underwriting
- Fidelity and surety bonding
- General insurance
- Insurance accounting and finance
- Insurance information technology
- Insurance production and agency management
- Insurance regulation and compliance
- Management
- Marine insurance
- Personal insurance
- Premium auditing
- Quality insurance services
- Reinsurance
- Risk management
- Surplus lines

Ethics—Ethical behavior is crucial to preserving not only the trust on which insurance transactions are based, but also the public's trust in our industry as a whole. All Institutes designations now have an ethics requirement, which is delivered online and free of charge. The ethics requirement content is designed specifically for insurance practitioners and uses insurance-based case studies to outline an ethical framework. More information is available in the Programs section of our website, www.TheInstitutes.org.

Flexible Online Learning—The Institutes have an unmatched variety of technical insurance content covering topics from accounting to underwriting, which we now deliver through hundreds of online courses. These cost-effective self-study courses are a convenient way to fill gaps in technical knowledge in a matter of hours without ever leaving the office.

Continuing Education—A majority of The Institutes' courses are filed for CE credit in most states. We also deliver quality, affordable, online CE courses quickly and conveniently through CEU. Visit www.CEU.com to learn more. CEU is powered by The Institutes.

College Credits—Most Institutes courses carry college credit recommendations from the American Council on Education. A variety of courses also qualify for credits toward certain associate, bachelor's, and master's degrees at several prestigious colleges and universities. More information is available in the Student Services section of our website, www.TheInstitutes.org.

Custom Applications—The Institutes collaborate with corporate customers to use our trusted course content and flexible delivery options in developing customized solutions that help them achieve their unique organizational goals.

Insightful Analysis—Our Insurance Research Council (IRC) division conducts public policy research on important contemporary issues in property-casualty insurance and risk management. Visit www.ircweb.org to learn more or purchase its most recent studies.

The Institutes look forward to serving the risk management and property-casualty insurance industry for another 100 years. We welcome comments from our students and course leaders; your feedback helps us continue to improve the quality of our study materials.

Peter L. Miller, CPCU
President and CEO
The Institutes

Preface

Agency Operations and Sales Management is the assigned textbook for the third course in The Institutes' Accredited Adviser in Insurance (AAI) designation program. The AAI program is designed to meet the educational needs of insurance producers, customer service representatives, and other agency personnel. The AAI program supports learner performance in three primary areas: (1) the technical aspects of the insurance industry, including coverage and pricing; (2) the marketing of insurance products, including producer relationships with clients and underwriters; and (3) the operation and management of insurance agencies and brokerages.

Agency Operations and Sales Management consists of three segments that group topics of a similar nature. Segment A, Principles of Agency Management, discusses topics including insurance agency formation, organizational management and agency sales management, and production planning. Segment B, The Insurance Production Enviroment, advances the discussion of producer-insurer relations, an agency's public image, the factors that contribute to agency growth and good customer communications, and market segmentation and target marketing. Segment C, Agency Management Tools and Processes, explores the various issues agency principals face when managing IT requirements, customer service, and agency finances.

The Institutes are thankful to the individuals who contributed to previous editions of the *Agency Operations and Sales Management* text as reviewers; advisory committee members; and, in particular, authors, including Peter R. Kensicki, DBA, CPCU, CLU, FLMI; Carol A. Hammes, CPCU; and Daniel P. Hussey, Jr., CPCU, AAI, ARM. For this edition, The Institutes would like to thank Cheryl Koch, CPCU, ARM, AAI; Catherine Zielinski; and Keith A. Boyer, ARM, AIC.

For more information about The Institutes' programs, please call our Customer Service Department at (800) 644-2101, email us at CustomerService@TheInstitutes.org, or visit our website at www.TheInstitutes.org.

Mary Ann Cook

Contributors

The Institutes acknowledge with deep appreciation the contributions made to the content of this text by the following persons:

Richard Berthelsen, JD, CPCU, AIC, ARM, AU, ARe, MBA

Pamela J. Brooks, MBA, CPCU, AAM, AIM, AIS

Douglas Froggatt, CPCU, AINS

Ann E. Myhr, CPCU, ARM, ASLI, AU, AIM, MS

Laura J. Partsch, JD

Judith M. Vaughan, CPCU, AIC

Contents

Direct Your Learning ▶▶

Agency Formation and Environment

Educational Objectives

After learning the content of this assignment, you should be able to:

▷ Describe the principal-agent relationship in terms of the following:

- Duties an agent owes to the principal

- Remedies a principal has for an agent's breach of duties

- Duties a principal owes to an agent

- Remedies an agent has for a principal's breach of duties

▷ Describe the insurance agency-principal relationship in terms of the following:

- The specific duties owed by insurance agents

- The difference between insurance agents and brokers

- The authority of insurance agents

▷ Describe producer licensing requirements.

▷ Describe the major sections of an insurance agency contract, including any supplemental agreements.

▷ Describe the following forms of legal ownership of an insurance agency and the advantages and/or disadvantages of each:

- Sole proprietorships

- Partnerships

- Corporations.

▷ Describe insurance agency operating affiliations in terms of the following:

- The various types of operating affiliations and how they can be formed

- The advantages and disadvantages of independent agency networks

- How to evaluate independent agency networks

1

- How to evaluate other support organizations that an agency might affiliate with

▶ Describe the purpose of each of the federal and state regulations governing insurance.

Agency Formation and Environment

AGENT'S DUTIES AND REMEDIES

In an agency relationship, the principal and agent have specific obligations to each other. If either party fails to fulfill these obligations and thereby harms the other party, legal remedies are available to allow the injured party to recover.

An agent's duties to a principal include loyalty, obedience, reasonable care, accounting, and information. If the agent fails to fulfill these duties, the principal can sue the agent to recover any resulting loss or damage.

The principal's duties to the agent include an agreed-on period of employment, compensation, reimbursement for expenses, and indemnity for losses. If the principal breaches these duties, the agent can sue or can retain the principal's property until the principal has paid the amounts due. See the exhibit "Defining Agent, Producer, and Broker."

Defining Agent, Producer, and Broker

In insurance, the term "agent" is used in a more specific manner than in general agency law. Agents representing insurance principals are generally referred to as producers. For purposes of this material, a producer is defined as an individual who sells insurance products and related services. The producer may be an agent—the authorized representative of an insurer—or a broker—the authorized representative of an insured. For simplicity, the producer's employer or office is called "the agency" throughout this material. As such, an independent agent in Pierre, South Dakota; a sales representative for a large direct writer; an exclusive insurer's agent in Belpre, Ohio; and a broker in New York City all work out of "an insurance agency," and all are producers.

[OV08172]

Agent's Duties to Principal

An agent's implied fiduciary duties to a principal include these:

- Loyalty
- Obedience
- Reasonable care
- Accounting
- Information

Violation of any of these duties subjects the agent to discharge and to liability for any damages to the principal even if the agency contract does not expressly state these duties.

A subagent, who is the agent of an agent, owes the same duties to the principal that the original agent owes. An original agent is responsible to the principal for any subagent's violation of duty, even if the agent has exercised good faith in selecting the subagent. Further, a subagent owes the agent who did the hiring substantially the same duties.

If a subagent is employed without a principal's authority, no agency relationship arises between the principal and the subagent. The principal is not liable to third parties for an unauthorized subagent's acts. At the same time, the unauthorized subagent owes no duties to the principal.

Loyalty

One of the agent's most important duties is loyalty to the principal's interests. The agent must not undertake any business venture that competes with or interferes with the principal's business.

The principal can claim any profits the agent realizes in dealing with the principal's property. For example, any gift the agent receives from a third party while transacting the principal's business belongs to the principal. The duty of loyalty, however, does not obligate the agent to shield a principal who is acting illegally or dishonestly. To illustrate, Jo learns that her principal, Pete, cheated Tom on various contracts that Jo had arranged between Pete and Tom. Jo can disclose Pete's actions to Tom. If Tom obtains a judgment against Pete for his improper dealings, Pete cannot recover from Jo for breach of the duty of loyalty. Jo's duty does not extend to concealing Pete's dishonest acts from persons those actions affect.

Obedience

An agent owes a duty to obey a principal's lawful instructions. If the agent disobeys a reasonable instruction, the principal can sue for any resulting damages and can also terminate the relationship. Generally, the agent cannot challenge the instruction, unless it calls for illegal or immoral acts.

The agent owes a duty to perform according to the principal's instructions. If the principal has given ambiguous instructions, the agent owes the duty to exercise his or her best judgment in carrying them out. However, if harm to the agent is possible, or if an emergency arises, the agent might be justified in disobeying the principal's instructions.

An agent cannot delegate the authority granted by a principal to another person. The principal selects the agent because of personal qualifications. However, three exceptions apply to the nondelegation rule:

- **Ministerial duties**—If certain tasks do not require judgment or discretion, an agent can delegate their performance.

- Customary appointments—If custom and usage of a particular business involve the delegation of authority, the agent can delegate.

- Emergency appointments—In an emergency that requires the appointment of another to protect the principal's interests, the agent can make an emergency appointment.

Ministerial duties
The routine or mechanical tasks performed by agents.

Reasonable Care

An agent must exercise the degree of care and skill that a reasonable person would exercise under the same or similar circumstances. An agent with special skills or training is held to the standard of care of a reasonable person possessing those skills. Thus, a real estate broker employed to sell property must exercise the reasonable care of any real estate broker dealing with similar property.

An agent's failure to act when action is reasonably required also constitutes a breach of this duty. An agency contract carries an implied promise that the agent will carry out the duties of the agency with reasonable care to avoid injury to the principal. To illustrate, Charles asks Marcie, an insurance broker, to obtain an automobile insurance policy with collision coverage for his car. Marcy obtains a policy and delivers it to Charles, but the policy does not include collision coverage. After Charles has an accident, he learns that no collision coverage is in force. Charles may have a **cause of action** against Marcie for breach of the duty of reasonable care.

Cause of action
A plaintiff's legal grounds to sue a defendant.

Reasonable care is required whether or not the agent is paid for the services. Unpaid agents cannot be compelled to perform duties, but once they begin performance, they are held to the standard of reasonable care. For example, real estate broker Betty gratuitously promises to act as Clark's agent in the sale of his real estate. Clark cannot sue Betty for her failure to try to sell the property. However, suppose Betty convinced Tony to purchase Clark's property and failed to have Tony sign a binding sales agreement. If Tony later declined to proceed with the purchase, Clark could sue Betty for negligence for her failure to exercise the degree of reasonable care.

An agent and a principal can agree that the agent is not to be liable to the principal for ordinary negligence. An agent, however, cannot evade liability for gross negligence. To limit the agent's liability for gross negligence would be against public policy.

Accounting

An agent must account to the principal for all the principal's property and money that come into the agent's possession. As part of this duty, the agent must keep the principal's property, including money, separate from the agent's. If the agent commingles the property or money, then the law assumes that it all belongs to the principal unless the agent clearly proves otherwise.

Money held by the agent should be deposited in a separate bank account in the principal's name. If the agent deposits it in his or her own name and the bank then fails, the agent is liable for any loss the principal sustains. The agent should account promptly for any of the principal's money held. Failure to do so makes the agent liable for interest payments to the principal.

Information

An agent owes a duty to keep the principal informed of all facts relating to the agency. Therefore, if a principal authorizes an agent to sell property for a specified amount and the agent later learns that the property's value has materially changed, then the agent must give the principal that information. Generally, the agent owes a duty to make reasonable efforts to provide the principal with information relevant to the affairs entrusted to the agent. Failure to perform this duty makes the agent liable to the principal for any resulting loss.

The law imputes the knowledge an agent obtains during the course of performing a principal's business to the principal and therefore imposes on the agent the duty to give the information to the principal. Most courts do not impose a duty to communicate information that the agent obtains outside the scope of the agent's employment. Additionally, if an agent acts adversely to the principal's interest, by colluding with a third party to defraud the principal, for example, that knowledge will not be imputed to the principal. See the exhibit "E&O Alert."

E&O Alert

All agencies share a framework of fundamental legal and business characteristics. The basic principles of agency formation, the agency relationship, and contracts form this framework. The framework illustrates certain unique characteristics that distinguish insurance agencies from other types of agencies. Operating within that framework and understanding the unique duties owed by an agent to his or her principal will reduce the number and severity of E&O claims an agent faces over a career.

[OV08173]

Principal's Remedies

Depending on the offense, a principal can sue an agent for breach of the agency contract or in tort for harm done. Remedies include requiring the agent to transfer improperly held property, pay the value of the benefit the agent received, or pay damages for negligence or tort.

If the agent is insolvent, the principal's best remedy is a suit to transfer the property. If the agent has personally profited from the transaction, then a suit for the value of the benefit the agent received represents the principal's best alternative. In other cases, a suit for breach of agency contract may be preferable to a suit in tort because the statute of limitations is generally longer for contract suits than for tort suits.

In still other cases, the principal can sue for an injunction prohibiting the agent from revealing trade secrets obtained during the course of employment or from competing with the principal in violation of a noncompetition agreement after termination of employment.

Principal's Duties to Agent

The principal owes these duties to the agent:

- Agreed-on period of employment
- Compensation
- Reimbursement for expenses
- Indemnity for losses

Agreed-On Period of Employment

Either party can terminate an employment contract at will unless the contract specifies a fixed period of employment. A contract to pay a salary by the month or year does not necessarily indicate that employment is guaranteed for the stated period.

A contract with a fixed period of employment makes the parties liable for any breach of their contract within that period. Because the agency relationship is consensual, the parties can refuse to continue the relationship during the contractual period, but they are subject to damages for breach of the contract.

When an employment contract provides for a specified period of employment and the principal's business terminates during the period, the agency also terminates because of changed conditions.

Compensation

The principal must pay the agent the agreed-on compensation for the services performed. If no compensation agreement exists, the agent is entitled to the reasonable value of the services rendered. If the contract does not mention compensation but an agent under similar circumstances would receive compensation for services, compensation is required for the reasonable value of the services. However, an agent who breaches agency duties is not entitled to compensation.

A principal is not responsible for a subagent's compensation if the agent was given no authority to hire subagents. Likewise, if the agent has the authority merely to delegate duties to a subagent, the agent, not the principal, is responsible for compensation.

Reimbursement for Expenses

A principal must reimburse an agent for any expenses necessarily incurred for the discharge of agency duties. For example, if the agent must incur travel and advertising expenses to accomplish agency purposes, the principal must reimburse these expenses. The agent must spend the money reasonably. If the agent's negligent conduct results in unnecessary expense, the agent bears the expense rather than the principal.

Indemnity for Losses

The principal owes a duty of indemnity, or reimbursement, for any losses or damages the agent has suffered because of the agency and incurred through no fault of the agent. If a principal directs an agent to commit a wrong against a third party, and the agent does not know that the act is wrongful, the agent is entitled to indemnity for the amount paid as a result of a lawsuit arising from the act. To illustrate, a principal directs an agent to cut down and sell trees on land that the principal incorrectly believes he owns. The landowner sues the agent to recover damages for loss of the trees. The agent is entitled to indemnity by the principal.

A principal must indemnify an agent for the expenses incurred in defending any lawsuits resulting from the agent's authorized acts. If the expense resulted from the agent's own intentional or negligent conduct, even though the principal directed the act, the agent is usually not entitled to indemnification. To illustrate, Paul promises to reimburse his sales representative, Anne, for money she pays out in illegal gratuities to purchasing agents to whom she sells goods. Anne is not entitled to indemnification from Paul for money she pays illegally.

An agent who makes payments or becomes subject to liability to third persons because of a subagent's authorized conduct has the same right to indemnity from the principal as if the conduct were the agent's. Because a subagent is both the agent's and the principal's agent, the subagent is entitled to indemnity from either of them.

Agent's Remedies

An agent can sue for compensation, indemnity, or reimbursement and can also obtain a court order requiring an accounting from the principal. An agent discharged by a principal during a specified employment period can sue for compensation for the remainder of the period.

An agent can also exercise a lien, or right to retain possession of the principal's goods, until the principal has paid the amounts due. Some agents, such as attorneys, bankers, and stockbrokers, can enforce a general lien against the principal; that is, they can hold the principal's goods and papers until all accounts are settled. The general lien is not limited to the immediate transaction between the parties but to all transactions between the agent and principal. Many other kinds of agents can assert only a special lien, which allows retention of the principal's property until the account for the immediate transaction between the principal and agent is settled.

INSURANCE PRODUCERS AND AGENCY LAW

Although the agent and principal relationship is based on concepts and legal doctrines that apply to all business agreements, there are many unique aspects of the relationship between insurers and their agents.

In the various insurance marketing systems, salespeople are generally called producers, agents, or brokers. However, most insurance customers refer to their sales representative as their agent.

All independent insurance agents operate under the law of agency. Although there are functional differences between agents, brokers, general agents, and so on, the law does not usually draw a significant distinction between the legal responsibilities of these individuals. The determining factor is not the name under which the producer operates, whether agent or broker or another term, but rather the type of activity in which the producer is engaged. The National Association of Insurance Commissioners (NAIC) has adopted this perspective in its Producer Licensing Model Act of 2000 (PLMA). The PLMA provides for a single producer license that authorizes all producers to broker insurance for insurers or as consumer representatives under selected lines of business, such as personal lines insurance, commercial lines insurance, property and casualty insurance, or surplus lines insurance. Ultimately, should a producer's activities lead to a lawsuit, the plaintiff has the burden of proof in establishing whether the insurance seller is an agent or a "broker in an insurance transaction,"[1] regardless of license type. Most states have adopted the model act or similar licensing legislation.

Duties of Insurance Agents

Insurance company agents owe the same duties to their principals as agents do in other businesses. These duties include loyalty, obedience, reasonable care, accounting, and the duty to give information. However, the duty of loyalty owed by the insurance agent raises some special considerations. Normally, a person who is employed by two parties to conduct a transaction between them (all facts being known to both parties) is the agent of both parties and owes a duty to each to deal fairly. This relationship, in which the agent represents both a buyer and a seller to conduct a transaction between them, is called **dual agency**.

Dual agency

A relationship in which the agent represents both a buyer and a seller to conduct a transaction between them.

E&O Alert

Dual agency is an unavoidable reality for insurance agents. If the agent is seen as unduly favoring either the insurer or the insured in a given situation, the slighted party may resort to an E&O claim to recover its loss.

[DA08154]

In a dual agency relationship involving insurance transactions, the agent may owe allegiance to two principals: as an agent for one principal for part of a transaction, and as a producer/agent for the other principal for the remainder of the transaction. For example, an insurance broker may be the insured's agent in securing a policy and, as is generally required by specific statute, may also be the insurer's agent in receiving premiums.

In the usual insurance company-agent relationship, courts tend to infer that the agent's fiduciary duties are owed to the insurer. Statutes in many states stipulate that insurance agents are agents of the insurer and not of the insured so that information given to the agent, or payment made to the agent, is binding on the insurer. Attempts by insurers to include contractual provisions that stipulate that the agent is the insured's agent have not been recognized by the courts.

A producer in a dual agency role might take a bargaining position between the insurer and the insurance buyer, but this is a difficult position to assume and to maintain with objectivity. Courts recognize the dual agency status of agents and brokers as an exception to the general rule of an agent's serving only one principal. The producer usually represents the insurer when binding insurance, keeping records, collecting premiums, and issuing and canceling policies. The producer usually represents the customer when suggesting and selecting coverages or insurers.

Agents and Brokers Compared

Whether an insurance producer is an agent or a broker depends on whose interests the producer represents. When representing the insurance buyer, the

E&O Alert

The independent agency and brokerage system puts the producer in a dual agency capacity. The independent agent has traditionally advertised service to the insurance buyer and yet is contracted to the other party to the transaction—the insurer. At various points in the transaction, the agent or broker will shift from representing one principal to representing the other principal. If you are an independent agent or broker, be careful not to violate your duties to either principal.

[DA08155]

producer is a broker. When representing the insurance seller (an insurer), the producer is an agent. Under the law of agency, the customer is the broker's principal, and the insurer is the agent's principal as illustrated in the exhibit. See the exhibit "Agent-Principal Relationship in Insurance Production."

Agent-Principal Relationship in Insurance Production

	Principal	Agent	Third Party
Brokerage	Customer ⟶	Broker ⟶	Insurer
Agency	Insurer ⟶	Agent ⟶	Customer

[DA08156]

However, strict application of the rule that brokers always represent insureds exclusively can lead to unjust results, penalizing the public for dealing with brokers while allowing insurers to escape responsibility for broker acts for which they should be responsible. Consequently, as a matter of consumer protection, most courts and state insurance regulators have taken the position that the broker can be considered an agent for the insurer as well as the insured's representative.

The nature of the circumstances, rather than the strict legal relationship of the parties, often determines whether the producer is considered the agent of the insurer or of the insured. For example, most states have laws that make the broker the insurer's legal agent for the purpose of premium collection. Additionally, if an insurer, through its dealings, allows a broker to act so that a reasonable third party believes the broker is the insurer's agent, then the broker is the insurer's agent under the law. Such laws permit the general public to rely on the certainty that payment to their insurance broker is payment to the insurer.

How authority is granted also may determine whether an agent represents the insurer or the insured. Insurers grant authority to their agents by an agency contract written and executed by both principal and agent. Brokers rarely enter into written agreements with insurance buyers, but it is good practice for a broker to have a written agreement covering any fees that a customer may be charged. Because the broker represents the insurance buyer, it is rare to find a written agreement granting binding authority between a broker and an insurer. A broker who places business regularly with an insurer may have a written agreement governing such matters as the terms of premium payment, but these brokerage agreements make it very clear that the broker is not an agent of the insurer.

Brokers are typically paid a commission, which is part of the insurance premium. In this regard, they are no different from agents who are paid a commission. Many brokers (especially when dealing with large commercial accounts) have moved away from traditional commission arrangements toward a fee system in which the customer pays for the broker's professional services in addition to paying the insurance premium to the insurer. When a broker charges a fee, the insurance is usually "written net" by the insurer; that is, the premium is reduced to eliminate the producer commission. The broker is then free to negotiate a fee based on the work to be performed, irrespective of the size of the insurance premium. This approach also helps the broker and the insurer comply with any laws that prohibit a producer from taking both a commission and a fee. The exhibit illustrates the commission and fee systems. See the exhibit "Commission and Fee Systems."

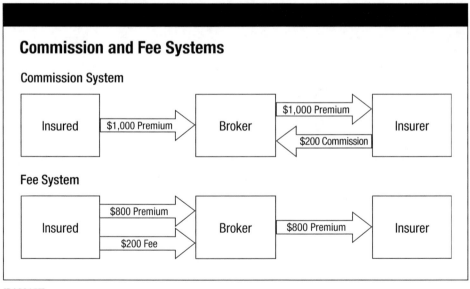

Commission and Fee Systems

Commission System

Insured — $1,000 Premium → Broker — $1,000 Premium → Insurer
                                Broker ← $200 Commission — Insurer

Fee System

Insured — $800 Premium → Broker
Insured — $200 Fee → Broker — $800 Premium → Insurer

[DA08157]

The fee system provides certain advantages for the broker. For example, the potential for conflicts of interest is minimized because the insurer does not pay a commission. Additionally, the fee can reflect the amount of compensation the broker requires for service, overhead, and profit. In a competitive market in which premiums (and therefore commissions) are shrinking, the broker's fee may remain constant or even increase.

The fee system also has a disadvantage for the broker. Fees are visible to the insurance buyer, whereas the commission is part of the premium. Knowing the fees that are charged, an insured can evaluate the cost of producer service separately from the cost of insurance protection and can negotiate the fee separately.

Marketing Tip—As commission levels that insurers pay to agents change (typically they decrease), many agents have begun looking at the fee system as a possible alternative. If a fee system still looks attractive to you after considering the pros and cons, be careful to review applicable state laws and regulations before implementing such a system. Some agents in some states may charge fees for additional services provided (such as risk management, claim, and loss control services) and collect these fees in addition to commissions. Even if the insured is fully aware of the fee and agrees to pay it, you may be conducting an illegal practice. Find out under what circumstances fees are allowed (if at all) and what disclosure arrangements are required in your marketing territory.

Authority of Insurance Agents

In the context of agency law, authority is the agent's legal power arising from the agency relationship. An agent's power to bind the principal is determined by the agent's authority, which is derived expressly, by implication, or from the facts of the situation. These types of authority are called, respectively, express authority, implied authority, and apparent authority. An agent's authority is also affected by ratification, if the agent is an independent contractor, and if the principal is undisclosed or nonexistent.

Express Authority

Express authority is conferred by a principal on an agent through specific instructions, and it includes the authority needed to carry out acts incidental to those instructions. An agent receives express authority through a legal agreement, either oral or written, granted by the principal. The law recognizes the following two degrees of agency, defined by the range of express authority granted:

Express authority
The authority that the principal specifically grants to the agent.

- A general agent has authority to perform all acts that are usual and customary in such a capacity. For example, a construction project general manager or a stockbroker managing an investment portfolio conducts a series of transactions for a principal on an ongoing basis.

- A special agent is usually restricted to performing just those acts essential to the situation. A special agent may conduct a single transaction or a small group of transactions for the principal on a limited-term basis, such as a stockbroker asked to purchase a certain number of shares in a specific company.

The terms "general agent" and "special agent" as used here should not be confused with the day-to-day use of these terms by producers. Most property-casualty insurance producers are general agents in the legal sense, with authority, within expressed limits, to make or to modify contracts of insurance and to perform all of the other activities necessary to the efficient operation of an insurance agency.

Every producer should be aware of the limits of the express authority granted by each insurer represented. Although express authority can be given through oral or written instructions, an insurer's instructions to an agent are usually written. They result from the negotiations that established the agency relationship or that modify it from time to time. The agency contract offered by an insurer and signed by the agency's owners contains express authority for the agency to represent the insurer. The sample agreement illustrates aspects of express authority in insurance agency contracts.

Insurance agency agreements define the agent's express authority in relation to binding and issuing policies, collecting and remitting premiums, and earning commissions. These definitions of authority are expanded by references to the law, to attached addenda or schedules, and to insurer underwriting rules—all of which explicitly limit agency authority. See the exhibit "Express Authority Sample."

Express Authority Sample

IT IS HEREBY AGREED between the Company and the Agent as follows: (1) The Company hereby grants authority to the Agent to receive and accept proposals for insurance and to issue contracts of insurance on policy forms provided by and at premium rates developed or adopted by the Company covering risks as authorized in the addenda attached hereto within the state of (name of state) subject, however, to restrictions placed upon the Agent by applicable state laws and to the terms and conditions hereinafter set forth and to such instructions as may be given to the Agent by the Company from time to time.

[DA08158]

Implied Authority

Implied authority

The authority implicitly conferred on an agent by custom, usage, or a principal's conduct indicating intention to confer such authority.

No agency contract can encompass every possible contingency. Therefore, the agreement is broadened by law and custom to include other acts deemed necessary to carry out the agent's express authority. In other words, the agent has implied authority to carry out the express authority. **Implied authority** is implicitly conferred on an agent by custom, usage, or a principal's conduct indicating the intention to confer such authority. It is within the scope of authority granted by a principal to an agent, even though not expressly granted. Implied authority cannot exist without express authority. For example, an insurance agent has the implied authority to advertise that he or she represents a certain insurer, even if the agency contract does not specifically state this. The right to advertise representation is implied because advertising is necessary to carry out the agent's commitment to solicit insurance on the insurer's behalf.

An agent should be able to believe that any actions made in accordance with accepted custom are within the scope of the authority granted. Usually, this authority is similar to that of other agents in similar positions. Implied authority is simple in principle but can cause problems in practice because it is vague. A producer who is in doubt about the extent of implied authority should ask the principal for clarification.

Implied authority also may arise from a principal's conduct that could be construed as intending to confer such authority. For example, if an insurance agent has for years been able to bind property submissions without limit on value, that agent has, by implication, the right to continue to do so until the insurer expresses otherwise.

E&O Alert

When, through any of its employees or solicitors, an insurance agency exceeds its express or implied authority from an insurer, the agency may be liable to both the customer and the insurer for financial loss caused as a result of the exceeded authority. Care should be taken that all personnel in the agency are well aware of their individual authority as well as the authority of the agency itself. Any unusual limitations on an agent's authority must be communicated to third parties, and the insurance producer operating under special limitations of authority must be careful not to exceed those limitations.

[DA08159]

Apparent Authority

Apparent authority is based on a third party's reasonable belief that an agent has authority to act on behalf of the principal and which the principal cannot therefore deny. It is often called authority by estoppel on the theory that if a principal creates the appearance of authority in an agent and a third party reasonably relies on that appearance, the principal should be estopped (prevented) from denying that authority.

Apparent authority is derived from the circumstances of the situation. Few members of the general public know the exact extent of the express and implied authority relationships between agents and their principals; therefore, the existence of apparent authority is determined by how a third party perceives the situation. If the third party perceives that the supposed agent has authority, the courts will hold the principal to obligations made by the supposed agent as long as the agent has operated according to the accepted customs and traditions of the business.

For example, suppose an unlicensed office employee of an insurance agency binds coverage while the licensed producers are away from the office. Because it would be reasonable for a member of the public to assume that the clerical person had the necessary authority to bind the coverage, the insurer would be held liable for the coverage even though an agent did not prepare the binder.

Apparent authority
A third party's reasonable belief that an agent has authority to act on the principal's behalf.

> **E&O Alert**
>
> In the preceding scenario, the insurer may have a right of action against the agency for any damages it sustains in paying the claims resulting from the coverage the clerical employee bound. Apparent authority, however, ensures that the public is still protected.

[DA08160]

The concept of apparent authority may appear to be unfair to the principal, but its result is to protect innocent third parties, allowing them to recover from the principal when the principal has made it appear, either intentionally or unintentionally, that the agent has authority to act.

Third parties, however, cannot depend so completely on appearances created by the agent that they are absolved of all responsibility to act as reasonable and prudent consumers. The public has a responsibility to protect itself and must always be alert to unusual situations. When an agent acts in a way that appears to be adverse to the best interests of the principal, the third party has a duty to determine the extent of the agent's authority by a direct inquiry to the principal.

Agency by Ratification

Ratification

Creation of an agency relationship resulting when a principal adopts the act of another who has purported to act for the principal and has neither power nor authority to perform the act for the principal.

In addition to entering into an agency contract, an agency and an insurer can create agency by **ratification**, a form of post-contract authority that results when the principal affirms a transaction that exceeds an agent's express or implied authority.

By acting to exceed the express or implied powers granted by the principal, the agent has, in effect, entered a contract with a third party on the agent's own behalf rather than on the principal's behalf. If, after such a transaction, the principal, with knowledge of the unauthorized act, ratifies (approves) the agent's conduct, it is as if such authority had been granted in the first place. The ratification could come about by a written confirmation or simply by the principal's not rejecting the transaction.

These five requirements must be met for a court to affirm agency by ratification:

- The agent must claim to act for the principal at the time of the original transaction.
- The principal must ratify the entire transaction.
- The principal must ratify before the third party elects to withdraw.
- The principal must have full knowledge of all of the facts.
- The transaction must be legal.

If all of these requirements are met, the principal is bound by the transaction, and the inception of the resulting contract dates from the time of the original contract. If the principal does not ratify the agent's act, the agent alone is liable on the specific contract not ratified. Other contracts in force with the insurer are unaffected.

For example, an agent's contract with an insurer expressly limits the agent's property insurance binding authority to $1,000,000 per building. An existing customer calls to ask for coverage on a newly purchased $2,000,000 building. The agent binds the coverage and then asks the insurer to honor the binder. The underwriter refers the agent's request to the insurer's home office, which agrees to honor the binder three days later. The binder is now ratified, and coverage is effective from the moment the agent originally bound coverage.

Agent as Independent Contractor

An independent contractor is a person (or an organization) hired to perform services without being subject to the hirer's direction and control regarding work details. If the person engaging the contractor begins to exert control over the contractor in the performance of the task assigned, the status of independent contractor may be lost, and the parties become employer and employee.

A principal dealing with an independent contractor has the advantage of avoiding liability for the actions of the independent contractor; whereas an employer is responsible for an employee's actions that are performed within the scope of the employment. For example, a principal is not responsible for accidents caused by independent contractors using their own automobiles. Using independent contractors instead of employees is one way to transfer some of the liability loss exposures (particularly tort and criminal liability) that can arise from the actions of employees.

Insurance agency contracts typically afford independent contractor status to the agency. A section entitled "Agent-Company Relationship" in a sample agency agreement establishes independent contractor status:

> "This Agreement is not a contract of employment, and nothing herein contained is construed to create the relationship of employer and employee between Company and Agent. The agent is understood to be an independent contractor and is free to exercise judgment and discretion regarding the conduct of business as Agent for Company."

These same provisions may apply to independent or exclusive agents.

Agent Acting for an Undisclosed Principal

In some agency relationships, the principal is undisclosed; that is, the principal asks the agent to act as if the agent were the principal. For example, assume a prospective land purchaser is afraid prices will dramatically increase if the owners know the prospective purchaser is in the market. The land purchaser can instruct the real estate agent to act as if he or she were the prospective purchaser, thereby hiding the true purchaser's (the undisclosed principal's) existence from the sellers.

When a third party deals with an agent for an undisclosed principal and later learns of the existence of the principal—for instance, when the principal attempts to back out of the contract—the third party has the choice of suing either the agent or the principal for performance on the contract. The agent is not absolved of responsibility for breach of contract.

Similar to an undisclosed principal, a principal can also be partially disclosed. The agent is instructed to acknowledge the principal's existence but withhold the principal's identity. The legal protection afforded to the third party is virtually the same as with an undisclosed principal; that is, if a breach occurs, the third party can sue either the principal or the agent.

Agent and a Nonexistent Principal

The term "nonexistent principal" is used when an agent gives a third party the impression that he or she is acting for a principal when, in fact, there is no principal. For example, assume the producer is presented with an unusual or difficult loss exposure, knowing it will have to be placed through Lloyd's of London. Suppose the producer says to the customer, "I'll insure you through Lloyd's." However, Lloyd's is not an insurer, but rather a specialist insurance market made up of members who underwrite in syndicates; therefore Lloyd's cannot be a principal. In this case, the producer is operating for a nonexistent principal and must bear any loss from the time the customer reasonably believes the coverage is in force until the underwriters at Lloyd's accept the submission.

PRODUCER LICENSING

Producers are required by state laws to be licensed in every state in which they do business. Recently, it has become easier to comply with these laws because of the National Insurance Producer Registry (NIPR).

State insurance laws prohibit insurers from giving any authority to unlicensed agents. Agency contracts reinforce this prohibition with wording that stipulates automatic termination of the agency if the agent's license is suspended, canceled, or nonrenewed.

Whether an insurance producer is called an agent or a broker, the laws of each state require testing and licensing before a producer can represent an insurer or an insured. Some states have several different licenses, such as those for surplus lines producers or for producers with major lines of authority in (property-casualty or life-health). Additionally, some states license claim representatives, while others license insurance consultants.

Producers who engage in insurance business without first complying with state licensing requirements are subject to prosecution and fines. A license does not prevent a policyholder from suing an agent or an insurer for an error or omission. Some errors and omissions policies have coverage limitations on payment if the agent is not properly licensed.

Producers

Producers must be licensed in each state where they do business. To obtain a license to sell a particular type of insurance, a producer must pass a written examination. Insurance producers operating without a license are subject to civil, and sometimes criminal, penalties.

Traditionally, lack of uniformity among the states' licensing requirements has been a source of frustration and an expense for producers licensed in more than one state. Provisions in the Gramm-Leach-Bliley (GLB) Act have led to greater licensing reciprocity among states. Regulators' ultimate goal is to move beyond reciprocity and to resolve issues related to uniformity in producer licensing. Meeting this goal will streamline the licensing process while retaining state regulatory authority over it.

Much progress has been made in recent years in addressing producer concerns about the lack of uniformity. The development of the NIPR has eliminated many of the inconveniences that arise from a multi-state regulatory system. The NIPR is a unique public-private partnership that supports the work of the states and the NAIC in making the producer licensing process more cost effective, streamlined, and uniform for the benefit of regulators, insurance producers, insurers, and consumers. The NIPR vision is to provide one place for producers to go to meet all aspects of the producer licensing and appointment process using an electronic communication network. The NIPR developed and implemented the Producer Database (PDB) and the NIPR Gateway.

- The PDB is an electronic database consisting of information relating to insurance producers that links participating state regulatory licensing systems into one common repository of producer information. The PDB also includes data from the NAIC Regulatory Information Retrieval System to provide a more comprehensive producer profile. Some of the key benefits of PDB are increased productivity, lower cost, reduction of paper, access to real-time information, and the ability to conduct national verification of the license and status of a producer.

- The NIPR Gateway is a communication network that links state insurance regulators with the entities they regulate to facilitate the electronic exchange of producer information. Data standards have been developed for the exchange of license application, license renewal, appointment, and termination information.

Claim Representatives

Some states require claim representatives to be licensed so that those who make claim decisions for insurers are aware of prohibited claim practices, have a minimum level of technical knowledge and skill, and understand how to handle insureds' claims fairly. Licensing of claim representatives in most states includes an examination, which is important because of the complex and technical nature of insurance policies and the claim process. The licensing process also typically involves a background check, as well as ethics requirements, to help protect consumers who file claims from unfair, unethical, and dishonest claim practices.

Public adjusters, who represent insureds for a fee, are generally required to be licensed to ensure technical competence and to protect the public.

Insurance Consultants

Insurance consultants give advice, counsel, or opinions about insurance policies. Some states require insurance consultants to be licensed, and requirements for a consultant's license vary by state. Separate examinations are usually required to be an insurance consultant in both life-health insurance and property-casualty insurance.

INSURANCE AGENCY CONTRACTS

This section considers the common features of typical agency contracts that property-casualty insurers offer to their independent contractor agents. Although contracts vary by insurer, certain topics are part of virtually every contract. Various industry groups have attempted to standardize insurance agency contracts for ease and consistency in doing business. For example, the Independent Insurance Agents and Brokers of America, Inc. (IIABA), has studied agency contracts and recommended certain criteria in The Independent Agent's Guide to Agency-Company Agreements[2], which forms the basis of the following discussion.

An insurer and an agency individually enter each contract, and the relative bargaining power of the two parties determines how extensively the contract offered by the insurer is modified to favor the agency. Producers seek as much authority as possible on the most favorable terms. Many insurers have several alternative standard contracts, and an assertive agent may be able to obtain a better contract than an agent who accepts an insurer marketing representative's first contract offer.

Agency agreements vary considerably and often alter the general duties of the principal and agent. Producers must understand the agency contract because the agency owner is liable for the conduct of producers, and a producer's act that is contrary to the agency contract could jeopardize that contract. A typical contract contains seven major sections, followed by commissions and/or contingent commission agreement schedules.

Major Sections of an Agency Contract

The order the major sections appear in an agency contract can vary according to the contract. In accordance with specific insurer-agency negotiations, some contracts contain additional sections, and some contracts may not contain all the sections discussed here. Agency principals should carefully read and have a thorough understanding of all contract provisions before entering into any insurer agreement.

The seven major provisions of agency contracts are:

1. The term of agreement/termination
2. Rehabilitation
3. Ownership of expirations
4. Payment procedures
5. Indemnification
6. Contract amendments
7. Miscellaneous provisions

Term of Agreement/Termination

The first major section of an agency contract is the term of agreement/termination. Many contracts set an indefinite term by allowing the insurer to terminate the contract for any reason as long as the specified notice is given. This approach may put the agent at a disadvantage by making it difficult to perform long-term planning with any assurance that the insurer will continue the relationship. Consequently, many agency contracts set a specific term, with automatic rollover/renewal, unless the agent violates the agreement. The contract should specify the types of agent violations that would permit the insurer to cancel it. For example, many contracts specify that if the agent loses his or her license, the insurer can cancel the contract.

The contract should prohibit terminations based on volume or mix of business placed with the insurer unless the insurer has clearly informed the agent of such requirements in writing sufficiently in advance of termination to allow the agency a reasonable chance of meeting the requirements. The contract should also preclude any such termination if failure to meet the requirements is caused by the insurer's underwriting practices.

Similarly, the contract should allow termination based on agency loss ratios only if the agency's tendency to write consistently poor business is documented over a period of years. Shock losses (catastrophes such as earthquakes and tornadoes) and uninsured motorist losses (clearly outside the underwriting control of the agency) should be excluded from the loss ratio calculations. If, after these considerations, the agency's loss ratio still appears unacceptable to the insurer, the contract should specify that the agency shall be notified and given a reasonable chance to improve before the contract is terminated.

Industry practice requires that a party canceling an agency contract must give 180 days' written notice that includes the specific reason(s) for the termination. The agency contract should include a reasonable exception that would allow a shorter period for notice if the agency has failed to pay premiums due the insurer. In this case, a contract might specify that the insurer should provide the agency adequate time (ten days after notification of the past due amounts, for example) to pay, and routine bookkeeping errors and legitimate disputes over amounts owed should not activate this exception.

Contract termination sections must also address what happens to the agency's customers who are currently insured by the terminating insurer when a contract is canceled. Because a key issue for independent agents is ownership/control of expirations, the insurer must nonrenew all the policies currently written for the agency's customers. However, such a mass nonrenewal may cause confusion and hardship for the individual insureds. To allow for a smooth transition for the insured from the terminating insurer to the new insurer chosen by the agency, contracts include a **run-off provision** that allows current customers' policies to be renewed for a specified period after the termination of the agency's contract. For example, all policies coming up for renewal within twelve months after the contract termination should be renewed for at least one additional year, assuming the insureds meet current underwriting conditions. The rate of commission and other policy terms would be the same as those in effect on the date of the agency termination. The agency would continue to have the responsibility to service such business.

Run-off provision

An insurer contract provision allowing current customers' policies to be renewed for a specified period after the termination of an agency's contract.

Run-off provisions are being increasingly complicated by the growing number of state or other governmental restrictions on policy terminations. What happens, for instance, if a regulation requires a policy to be renewed beyond the period agreed to by the agency and insurer in the contract? The agency contract has been terminated, but the insurer must legally keep the policy in force. The agency, of course, wants to retain control/ownership of the expiration. Because the regulation is beyond the control of either the insurer or the agency, one compromise would be a provision continuing a limited agency contract only for policies affected by the regulation. This provision would grant the agency control of the policy whether or not it is ultimately continued in force with the current insurer. Without such a provision, an insurer may intend to move a policy to another of its agents for servicing, in effect assuming ownership of the expiration.

Rehabilitation

The second major section of an agency contract is rehabilitation. Assuming that contract termination is always the least favorable resolution to an agency's failure to fulfill an insurer's requirements, a rehabilitation clause provides for a period during which the agency can work to avoid termination. The insurer agrees to make a good faith effort to determine with the agency exactly what the agency must do to retain the contract. Although the period for the rehabilitation is negotiable, an agency should request a minimum of one year.

Ownership of Expirations

The third major section of an agency contract is ownership of expirations. Although customers are the only ones who truly control or "own" their policies and direct with whom they are insured, in any contract between an insurer and an agency, a key provision is which party has the right to control the relationship with a customer. Especially in today's evolving marketplace, in which many insurers are dealing directly with customers, both the insurer and the agency must clearly understand who has the final word on customer communications and solicitations.

In the case of agents who represent one insurer exclusively, the insurer often owns the expirations, not the agent. But for independent agencies, ownership of policy expirations determines whether an agency is truly independent. Although commissions on the sale of products are the major ongoing income source, the long-term value of the agency—the price at which it can be purchased or sold, or its value when passed on to heirs—is based on control and ownership of the book of business. Any restrictions or limitations on such control reduce the agency's value.

Agency ownership of its book of business is well established by court cases, but the specific wording in contracts often varies. Some insurers require joint ownership of expirations. Some contracts allow insurers to claim ownership from the agency if the contract is terminated for certain reasons. Other contracts require the agency to give the insurer a security interest in the expirations. These provisions are included in contracts to ensure payment of all premiums due the insurer. Ideally, from the agency's perspective, the contract should avoid limitations and should recognize the independent agency's clear and complete ownership of expirations under all circumstances.

Payment Procedures

The fourth major section of an agency contract is the payment procedures. The provisions of a contract between the agency and insurer must clearly delineate procedures for collecting and remitting money arising from the sale of insurance products, who is responsible for billing the customer, and how and when the billing party disburses to the nonbilling party the funds to which it is entitled.

When the agency sends premium bills to the insured, collects the premium, and sends the premium, less any applicable commission, to the insurer, the billing for that policy is typically referred to as being on an **agency bill** basis (sometimes called statement billing). The insurer submits a billing for its share of the premiums to the agency, usually on a monthly cycle. The agency, after verifying the accuracy of the insurer's billing, pays it. Although this billing method is typically used with large commercial accounts, some agencies prefer agency bill on as much of their business as possible because it gives them control of the funds and possibly significant investment income on the premiums invested between the date collected and the date paid to the insurer.

Agency bill

A payment procedure in which a producer sends premium bills to the insured, collects the premium, and sends the premium to the insurer, less any applicable commission.

Direct bill

A payment procedure in which the insurer assumes all responsibility for sending premium bills to the insured, collecting the premium, and sending any commission payable on the premium collected to the producer.

Another payment procedure is **direct bill**, in which the insurer sends the premium bills to the insured, collects the premium, and sends any commission payable on the premium collected to the producer. The agency's commissions are usually remitted on a monthly cycle. Nearly all personal insurance business is direct billed, and a growing percentage of small and medium commercial business is moving to this method.

The agency contract should address billing issues by clearly answering several questions. Which types of business will be put on direct bill and which on agency bill? For agency bill, when will the premiums be due for new business, renewals, and changes or endorsements? Will the agency collect the first premium payment on a direct billed policy? How prominently will the agency name be displayed on direct bill communications with an insured? Will copies of all direct bill communications of any type be furnished to the agency before being sent to the customer? Will the insurer accept all responsibility for potential errors and omissions arising from direct bill procedures? If the contract is terminated, will the insurer supply the agency with a complete list of all direct billed policyholders, their expiration dates, and necessary policy details?

Indemnification

The fifth major section of an agency contract is a provision dealing with indemnification in the event of an error and omissions claim. The contract should clearly delineate when the insurer will indemnify or defend the agency or hold the agency harmless if the claim arises solely or partially through the insurer's error.

An agency should avoid any contract clause that bases insurer indemnification of the agency on a contributory negligence liability standard. Contributory negligence means that an individual who contributes to his or her own injury should not recover damages for that injury. A contract clause might state, for example, that the insurer will indemnify the agency only for claims "caused solely and directly by error or omission of Company." With this wording, if the agency is even 1 percent at fault, the insurer has no obligation to indemnify the agency for any of the claim.

A fairer method on which to base insurer indemnification of the agency is to use a comparative negligence standard. This standard holds the agency responsible for its percentage of responsibility for the claim and holds the insurer responsible for the remainder. For example, in a contract using the comparative negligence standard, the insurer might agree to indemnify the agency for any "company act or omission, except to the extent the agent has caused such error." Under this standard, if the agency is found 1 percent at fault, the insurer will still indemnify and defend for the other 99 percent of the claim. State laws vary in their definitions of comparative negligence and in how the concept is applied.

Defense of E&O claims is just as important as indemnification for them. An agent should verify whether the contract requires the insurer to provide legal defense for the agent in an E&O claim. If not, the agent should make sure that E&O coverage is adequate for this purpose.

Some contract indemnification clauses impose certain requirements on the agency's E&O insurance coverage, such as participating in formal E&O loss control training or maintaining policies and procedures. Such requirements should be specific and reasonable, and the agency should agree to them only if compliance is practical and possible.

Contract Amendments

The sixth major section of an agency contract is contract amendments. Because the agency's ability to establish long-term plans is based on the stability of its contracts, the ease and frequency of amending the terms are vital. Although an agency and an insurer may agree to amend a contract at any time, many contracts allow the insurer to amend—with an average of ninety days' advance notice—regardless of the agency's consent. If such unilateral changes are made on short notice, particularly in such areas as commission schedules, they can have a financial effect on the agency.

If the contract allows the insurer to make changes unilaterally, the agent should seek a revised provision allowing for amendment by mutual agreement to give the agency longer notice of changes. Additionally, 180 days' minimum advance notice could be requested. To assist the agency with its financial planning, the agency may also seek a provision that any changes to commission schedules should remain in effect for at least twelve months. Ideally, the contract should require that all amendments be made only with the agreement of the agency and the insurer.

Miscellaneous Provisions

The seventh major section of an agency contract is the miscellaneous provisions section. This section contains provisions relating to arbitration and to the procedures to follow upon sale of the agency.

The **arbitration clause** provides a formal method for the agency and insurer to resolve disagreements arising under the agency contract. The parties should first make good faith efforts to settle any disagreements, but, if they fail, an arbitration agreement is often a cost-effective alternative to litigation or contract termination. Generally, the rules of the American Arbitration Association (AAA) are followed, whereby each party selects an independent representative, called an arbitrator. These two arbitrators then agree on a third arbitrator to avoid tie decisions. The decision of the arbitrators is then binding and final on both the agency and the insurer. The agency and the insurer bear equal costs for the proceeding, unless one of these parties is found by the arbitrators to have acted in bad faith.

Arbitration clause

A clause in an agency contract that provides a formal method for the agency and insurer to resolve disagreements arising under the contract.

Another important miscellaneous provision deals with procedures to follow upon sale of the agency. When an agency is sold, the buyer may be basing a percentage of the agency's value on the insurer's extending its contract to the new owner. The contract may specify that the insurer must be given reasonable notice of any impending sale, and if the insurer does not plan to appoint the new owner as an agent, the insurer will at least continue the contract for a specified time to allow the new owner to move the business to another insurer.

Commissions

Commissions are detailed in a schedule, which may be either part of the contract or a separate agreement. If provided in a separate agreement, the provisions for changing the schedule follow the same guidelines as previously discussed for the contracts themselves. Requiring a minimum twelve-month interval before a given commission rate can be changed gives some stability to the agency's financial planning.

Commission rates vary by type of insurance. For example, the rate may be relatively low (such as 2 percent) for large workers compensation accounts and at their highest (often 30 percent) for bonds. To keep premiums competitive, the rates for preferred types of policies may be lower than for standard or specialty products.

Management Tip—Agents should be aware that commission schedules may be negotiable with certain insurers. Because commissions form the backbone of agency income, completely understanding commission schedules and their possible variations is crucial.

Commission rates can also vary by agency. An agency that can deliver the business an insurer prefers in terms of markets, spread of business, volume of business, loss ratios, or other aspects may be in an excellent position to negotiate a higher commission schedule. The agency should be certain to discuss with the insurer exactly what criteria will lead to a better commission schedule. Conversely, the agency should also learn what criteria or actions will lead the insurer to lower commission rates.

Contingent Commission Agreements

Insurers sometimes provide contingent commission agreements as a form of incentive compensation for producers who exceed established benchmarks for profitability and volume of business. Agreements to award contingent commissions are known by several names, including profit sharing agreements, incentive commissions, placement service agreements, and market service agreements. However, contingent commission is the most frequently used term and is the term used in this discussion.

Contingent commission agreement

A contract provision in which an insurer agrees to make supplemental payments to producers based on profitability alone or on a combination of profitability, volume, and growth in the agency's book of business placed with that insurer.

A **contingent commission agreement** is a contract provision in which an insurer agrees to make supplemental payments to producers based on profitability alone or on a combination of profitability, volume, and growth in the agency's book of business placed with that insurer. The supplemental payments issued are not uniform, and not all insurers offer contingent commission agreements. However, contingent commissions can contribute significantly to agency revenues. For agencies that provide insurers with a steady stream of profitable business, these bonuses can provide up to 10 percent or more of total agency revenues.

Some of the factors to be considered by a producer negotiating a contingent commission agreement include the qualifying volume requirement; the lines of insurance that are included and excluded; how the insurer calculates income; how losses are defined; whether a stop loss provision applies to exclude claims over a certain dollar amount; how profit is to be calculated; and when profit sharing commission will be paid to the agency. Other considerations include whether the commission is subject to arbitration and what happens if the agency contract is terminated.

Changing market conditions make it difficult for agencies to determine the best contingent commission agreement option. Agreements based on premium volume, for example, deliver exceptional bonuses in a hard market with rising prices, but a soft market of dwindling premiums could result in no bonus (because of decreasing premium and an increasing loss ratio) despite the producer's working much harder to keep the business on the books. If an agency's poor loss ratio is at least partly the result of insufficient pricing and underwriting by the insurer, should the agency's bonus suffer? When a market (such as workers compensation) delivers high premiums but involves claim costs that are often beyond the agency's or insurer's control, should that type of insurance be included in or excluded from profitability calculations?

Because of these and many other questions, insurers and agents should regularly review contingent commission agreements in an ongoing effort to provide the optimal mix of reward and incentive intended. Additionally, for agencies that participate in contingent commission agreements, the IIABA, the NAIC, and other industry governing bodies recommend full disclosure of payment arrangements between insurers and producers and between producers and their customers.

LEGAL FORMS OF ORGANIZATION

In forming an agency, the principal selects the agency's legal form of business organization. Selecting the legal form that matches the agency's structure and daily operations and that best suits both the business and its owners can help the agency reach its goals.

The legal forms of business organization are sole proprietorships, partnerships, and corporations.

Sole Proprietorships

Sole proprietorship

A form of business in which one person owns the business assets and is personally liable for the business's debts.

A **sole proprietorship** is a business owned by a single individual who assumes all personal liability for the business. An advantage to sole proprietorships is that profits are included in the owner's income and not taxed separately. Sole proprietorships also have limited capital requirements and require a minimum degree of legal formality to establish themselves as a new business. The only requirements that must be met for operating an insurance agency as a sole proprietorship are obtaining a license issued by the state insurance regulatory authority and, in most jurisdictions, making a filing in compliance with fictitious trade name regulations if the sole proprietor's name is not the name under which the agency is to be operated.

Kathy Adams, operating Adams Insurance Agency as a sole proprietor, would have to register the name Adams Insurance Agency. Legally, the sole proprietorship would be referred to as Kathy Adams d/b/a (doing business as) Adams Insurance Agency. Kathy can then operate during hours she chooses, be her own boss, and know that her hard work is going directly into building her own business.

Being on one's own in business has its inherent disadvantages as well. For example, when an insurance agency, or any type of business, is operated as a sole proprietorship, the legal entity literally lives and dies with the owner; if the owner dies or becomes seriously disabled, the enterprise is terminated by operation of law. A sole proprietor like Kathy Adams can make provisions in advance for the sale of the business if she dies, becomes disabled, or wants to retire. Legally, however, the firm of Kathy Adams d/b/a Adams Insurance Agency ceases with the death of Kathy Adams.

Other disadvantages of the sole proprietorship as a form of business include unlimited personal liability for debts and judgments arising from the firm's operation, difficulty in raising capital, and the uncertainty of future employment for the employees and producers who are associated with, but are not owners of, the firm. Also, the pressure of management responsibilities on a sole proprietor running a business can be substantial. Payrolls have to be met, high quality employees must be retained, creditors must be paid, and customers must be satisfied.

Despite these disadvantages, thousands of insurance agencies operate successfully as sole proprietorships in the United States. Many firms begin as sole proprietorships and later change legal form to a partnership or corporation for the reasons discussed in the following sections.

Partnerships

Partnership

A for-profit business entity jointly owned by two or more persons who share ownership and profits (or losses), although not necessarily on an equal basis.

A **partnership** is a voluntary association of two or more persons who are co-owners of a business and who agree to share in its profit and/or losses. For instance, if Kathy Adams decides that operating an insurance agency alone is hindering her ability to make a profit, she might decide to join forces with

Bob Jones to form Adams & Jones Insurance Agency. As with sole proprietorships, partnerships are not taxed separately and are relatively easy to establish. The only requirements for an insurance agency partnership are the necessary insurance licenses and the filing of the fictitious name with the state government. In this case, the name would be Kathy Adams and Bob Jones d/b/a Adams & Jones Insurance Associates. The partners may not even realize that they have created a partnership as a legal business form.

In a partnership, every partner has a fiduciary relationship with the other partners and with the business. Fiduciary duties impose a high degree of mutual trust, loyalty, and good faith on the partners just as they do on agents or trustees. A partner's fiduciary duties are implied in law, and no contract can waive them.

Partnership agreements should clearly inform all partners of their rights and obligations in operating the firm and should include provisions for an orderly transition in the event of the death, disability, or retirement of one or more of the partners. Some very large entities, such as law firms or public accounting firms, continue as partnerships in spite of their size. In the case of insurance agencies, once firms reach a size at which the partnership becomes difficult to manage, incorporation generally follows.

A partnership has some of the disadvantages of a sole proprietorship, such as limited duration depending on the partners' health and life, and unlimited personal liability of each partner—even for the acts of the other partner(s). By law, a partnership terminates on the death or, possibly, the disability of any of the partners. A formal partnership agreement usually provides for the automatic creation of a new partnership consisting of the remaining partners on the death, disability, or retirement of a partner. Raising capital and sharing management responsibilities are easier in a partnership than in a sole proprietorship, but the security of the employees does not increase to any great extent as compared with a sole proprietorship. Many insurance agencies operate successfully as partnerships, with gradual changes in ownership as new partners join or as partners depart through retirement or death.

A partnership can be either a general partnership or a limited partnership. In a general partnership, all the owners are general partners with all the rights and obligations of a partner who operates the enterprise. A limited partnership includes at least one general partner and at least one limited partner, although there can be many partners in either category. The advantage of being a limited partner is that the maximum personal liability of each limited partner is the value of the capital invested by that partner. However, federal income tax laws still treat the limited partnership as a partnership.

As an illustration of a limited partnership, assume Kathy Adams and Bob Jones decide they require additional capital in their firm to continue to expand. They approach Jack Brown, one of their major customers, and he agrees to invest funds in the agency but wants to act only as a limited (that is, only a financial, "silent," or "money") partner because he is not going to be active in running the business and does not want to share Kathy's and Bob's unlimited personal liability for the partnership activities. The firm continues to do business as Adams & Jones; however, it may have to amend its fictitious name filing (and possibly insurance licenses) to reflect the new ownership. The limited partnership form of business enables a firm to raise capital from outside investors who are assured of limited personal liability as long as they are not active in the business.

Corporations

The three types of corporations are corporations, S corporations, and limited liability companies.

Corporation

An entity organized under law and entitled to the same rights as a person, distinct from its owners.

State government activates a corporation by issuing a charter to the incorporators. The **corporation**, once chartered, becomes a legal entity in and of itself. Its owners are called stockholders, and it is managed by a board of directors elected by the stockholders. A corporation has a life beyond that of its owners and is unaffected by the owners' disability or death. The ownership of a corporation is through shares of stock that can be given away, sold, or willed. The corporation offers limited liability to all owners, similar to that afforded to limited partners, so that the maximum that corporation owners stand to lose is their investment.

To continue the example of Adams & Jones Insurance Agency, suppose that the three owners decide to form a corporation. They would have to petition their state government for a charter, and, once it was granted, the state would create Adams & Jones Insurance Agency, Incorporated. Kathy Smith, Bob Jones, and Jack Brown would become stockholders in the corporation.

The amount of stock each holds would be determined by the size of their investments in the initial firm and the strength of their respective bargaining positions when they incorporated. The stockholders can easily transfer their own stock as they see fit. Most closely held corporations (those owned by only a few stockholders), such as Adams & Jones Insurance Agency, Inc., have a written buy and sell agreement giving surviving stockholders the right and obligation to acquire the stock of a departing stockholder.

Advantages of insurance agency incorporation include the limited personal liability it offers owners for the corporation's contracts and torts, an unlimited corporate lifespan, and the separate legal entity status. Further, the corporate legal form may make it easier to obtain capital because corporations can issue shares.

Disadvantages of the corporation as a legal form are the additional work required to comply with each state's general corporation law, the costs required to file articles of incorporation with the appropriate entity of the state in which the corporation is domiciled, and the time and expense required to document the activities of the corporation, including maintaining a board of directors, holding annual stockholders' meetings, and maintaining separate books and records from those of its shareholders/owners. Corporations are also taxed separately.

An **S corporation**—named after a section (Subchapter S) of the federal Internal Revenue Code (IRC)—is any small business corporation with 100 or fewer stockholders that provides limited liability to its owners and is subject to tax treatment similar to that of a sole proprietorship or a partnership. Whether a corporation should elect to be taxed as a corporation or as a partnership is a question for the tax adviser for that firm. In the example, Adams & Jones Insurance Agency, Inc., could elect to be an S corporation for income tax purposes. However, complying with a government's S corporation laws can be time consuming and expensive.

Another type of corporation, the **limited liability company (LLC)**, is a type of business that limits the liability of its owners or members (like a corporation) and that pays taxes only on its profits (like a partnership). LLCs are created under state laws with specific tax and liability provisions; owner/members may be relieved from personal liability like a corporation's owners and choose to be taxed like a partnership. LLCs have three major features:

- For federal and most state taxes, the LLC is treated as a partnership (with more tax flexibility than an S corporation).

- The personal assets of the members are shielded, as in a regular corporation, from the LLC's liabilities and obligations.

- LLCs have substantial flexibility in management arrangements and sharing of economic benefits among the members.

LLCs, created under state laws, must have a minimum of two members. If a sole proprietor wanted to take advantage of becoming an LLC, another person could be brought into the company to meet the member requirements. The tax advantages, flexibility in sharing economic benefits, liability protection for members' personal assets, and various other features have helped the LLC replace general partnerships, limited partnerships, and S corporations as the business structure of choice for closely held enterprises. This form of corporation is popular with service businesses, such as engineering, real estate, and investment firms, as well as insurance agencies. A concern, however, is the work and costs incurred to comply with a state's limited liability corporation laws. See the exhibit "Advantages and Disadvantages of Organizational Forms."

Choice of Legal Form

Choosing a legal form for an insurance agency is complex and requires the advice of legal and accounting experts. Although this is an important business decision for the agency owners, it has relatively little to do with the agency's day-to-day operations and is probably of little concern to the insurers represented by the agency or to the agency's customers. The existence of the agency does not automatically disclose the business form, and some states do

S corporation

A small business corporation restricted to no more than 100 stockholders that elects to be taxed under Subchapter S of the Internal Revenue Code. A Subchapter S corporation provides limited liability to its owners and tax treatment similar to that of a partnership. Profits, losses, and other tax items are passed through to the shareholders and are taxable to them on their individual returns.

Limited liability company (LLC)

A form of business entity that provides its owners the limited liability of a corporation and the tax advantages of a partnership.

Advantages and Disadvantages of Organizational Forms

Organizational Form	Advantages	Disadvantages
Sole Proprietorships	• Limited capital requirements • Not taxed separately • Minimum degree of legal formality • Be his/her own boss	• Agency lives and dies with owner • Unlimited personal liability for debts • Difficulty raising capital • Uncertainty of future employment for employees • Pressure on sole proprietor of management responsibilities
Partnerships	• Not taxed separately • Minimum degree of legal formality • Easier to raise capital than sole proprietorship • Sharing of management responsibilities • Limited liability if a limited partner	• Limited duration depending on partners' health • Unlimited personal liability for debts, even if incurred by another partner
Corporations	• Corporation has a life beyond its owners • Easier to obtain capital than partnership • Stockholders can easily transfer their stock • Limited liability to owners	• Work and costs to comply with state's general corporation law • Corporate earnings taxed separately
S Corporations	• Limited liability to owners • Not taxed separately	• Work and costs to comply with state's S corporation law
Limited Liability Corporations	• Limited liability to owners • Not taxed separately • Flexibility in sharing economic benefits	• Work and costs to comply with state's limited liability corporation law

[DA08161]

not require that corporations identify themselves as such by using the words "Incorporated" or "Inc." in the name of the firm. However, the nature of a firm's ownership may be identified in the fictitious-name filing made with the state, notice of which is published in a newspaper in the county in which the firm is located. The legal form chosen by an insurance agency, or by any other kind of enterprise, depends on such issues as the extent of personal liability the owners are comfortable with, continuity requirements of the business, the owners' desire to control the business, taxation, and the business's overall goals.

OPERATING AFFILIATIONS

Operating affiliations help the agency attain its goals by reaching additional customers and prospects, taking advantage of new marketing opportunities, and realizing economies of scale. An agency can affiliate with several diverse entities, but this discussion concerns only certain common opportunities available to an agency for affiliation. Trade associations such as IIABA and the National Association of Professional Insurance Agents (PIA) and professional associations like the CPCU Society are not considered in this context.

Although trade organizations and professional organizations are excellent resources for the agency, they are not founded primarily to assist a particular agency in reaching its production and financial goals. In contrast, these operating affiliations contribute to the competitive stance of an agency by providing services to the agency or making competitive products available to it:

- Independent agency networks
- Insurance company affiliations
- Specialty marketing groups
- General purpose groups
- Common identity groups

Independent Agency Networks

The idea of agents grouping together—networking—to share services and insurers is not new. However, recent interest in networking has been fostered by agencies' need for information technology (IT) systems and an awareness of the special treatment insurers offer to large agencies. An **independent agency network** is a group of agencies that contractually link to share services, resources, and insurers to gain advantages normally available only to large regional and national brokers. Independent agent networks are also known as agent groups, agent clusters, or agent alliances. They have been likened to the professional association arrangement in the medical field. Network members share support services and often physical space, but each

Independent agency network

A group of agencies that contractually link to share services, resources, and insurers to gain advantages normally available only to large regional and national brokers.

member of the group, or cluster, retains ownership of the member's individual book of business.

A network differs from a merger in that (1) a separate entity, the network, is created—usually as a partnership or corporation—in which shares of stock are owned by network agencies, and (2) ownership of policy expirations remains separately with the participating agencies.

The network's form and function can vary greatly depending on the needs of the members. Networks range from a collection of agents cooperating to penetrate a specific market segment to an arrangement that closely resembles a full-scale merger.

Advantages of Networks

Advantages of a networking arrangement include these:

- Network members often receive special treatment from their insurers because of their combined premium volume.

- Network members have greater influence for negotiating agency-company contracts. Some network members report a 2 to 3 percent increase in average commissions. For members who have fallen behind in information technology (IT) because of limited resources based on individual agency circumstances, the network arrangement can provide the impetus and funding to upgrade to a more productive agency management system.

- Insurers deal with one entity instead of several and realize economies and efficiencies in communication and work flow.

- A network can bring specialists together to form a new entity that can better serve customer needs and provide expertise in a variety of coverage areas.

- For the entrepreneur who values independence, the network provides an alternative to merging or selling the agency.

- Many agents report that they enjoy delegating personnel administration and other management tasks to an operations manager and returning to selling.

- The network arrangement can provide economies in physical space, staffing, and insurer relations.

- Advertising expenditures can be pooled effectively.

- A network can provide a trial period for agents who have reservations about whether a merger is appropriate for them.

Disadvantages of Networks

Networks may present these disadvantages:

- Independent businessowners may have difficulty agreeing on agency management issues. An individual who has successfully built an agency may not want to share decisions that affect that business.

- Network members must share financial information with one another. Loss of privacy in financial matters may make many businessowners uncomfortable.

- Members lose direct personal control of agency cash flow.

- Most networks report the necessity of hiring an operations manager, and some agents may have difficulty delegating the administration of the agency.

Forming a network requires patience and perseverance, attendance at many meetings, and a tolerance for members who may lose interest in the project. For agency owners who are used to taking decisive action, the process often moves too slowly.

Evaluating Independent Agency Networks

As agencies determine whether to join independent agency networks, they perform these five activities:

1. Develop a questionnaire
2. Inventory insurers
3. Decide whether to move
4. Appoint start-up committees
5. Decide on a structure for the board of directors

First, it is helpful when deciding whether to join a network to develop a questionnaire profiling potential network members. Drafted by the group, the questionnaire should focus on the information agents want to know about each other, such as business mix, premium income, numbers of accounts, commission income, percentage of direct-billed business, information technology (IT) capabilities, staffing, plans for perpetuation, areas of specialization and expertise, agency goals, loss ratios, areas of interest to the agency principals, and level of commitment toward beginning a network. This process of self-analysis can be a revealing and useful exercise in itself.

Second, interested agents should inventory the insurers that potential members represent and the products those insurers offer. All members must objectively analyze the insurers they represent because all members of the network will represent the insurers they decide to retain. This analysis allows the members to keep the insurers that will do the best job for the network and terminate the rest.

Third, participating members should decide whether to occupy the same building or whether the network should be established as a separate entity apart from member offices. Consolidating offices is not essential. The decision about whether to occupy one building should be made based on the group's goals. For example, if the group's primary interest is to consolidate space, supplies, and overhead, a physical move would achieve that. However, if the intent of networking is to present an image of an agency with a variety of servicing locations, a physical move is neither necessary nor desirable.

Fourth, start-up committees should be appointed. Separate committees might address these issues:

- Resources. This committee reviews the profile questionnaires and determines the seriousness and level of commitment of potential network members. The committee also analyzes the potential members' IT systems, staff, capital, and other resources.
- Finance. This committee analyzes financial statements, searches for start-up capital, and projects cash flow and costs for the new network.
- Management. This committee develops an organizational chart and investigates alternatives for the network's legal structure.
- IT. This committee assesses the members' strengths, weaknesses, existing systems, and future technology needs.
- Personnel. This committee evaluates the needs of the emerging network and analyzes the talents and training of existing employees.

Fifth, the structure of the agency network's board of directors should be decided. Many network arrangements have a "one agency, one vote" rule, regardless of the member agencies' size. Other networks rotate the leadership position among members so that each member has the chairman position at some time. The members must also decide how new members can join the network.

Insurance Company Affiliations

Insurers form networks of affiliated agencies for the purpose of marketing specialized products, such as group commercial or personal insurance. The benefit to the producer of affiliating with an insurer's marketing organization is that the producer gains access to an exclusive product of the insurer that is not available to other agents. Usually, these insurer marketing organizations are set up for mass marketing programs to industry trade groups, and the insurers create the sales opportunity by directly soliciting the group or by underwriting it for one of their agents (often called an originating agent), who agrees to permit the network to make the direct sales.

When a producer affiliates with an insurer in this way, the insurer often grants territorial exclusivity, a right that prevents other agents from accessing sales opportunities in a defined territory. The insurer provides leads to the agency, which is responsible for the sales and service aspects of the transaction. This affiliation can be a productive source of sales opportunities if the mass marketing programs are good ones. However, independent producers sometimes resist the degree of sales management the insurer exercises. They may understand the purpose for it, but the practical day-to-day requirements cause difficulties for producers who are used to controlling their own activities. Many agents affiliate defensively to prevent their competitors from acquiring the affiliation.

Specialty Marketing Groups

Specialty marketing groups are also mass marketing-oriented and involve a network much like the networks sponsored by insurers. The differences are that these groups are independently owned and the programs are underwritten by more than one insurer. ARM (Associated Risk Managers) International and MMI (Marketing Management, Incorporated) are examples of specialty marketing groups.

As with insurer-sponsored affiliations, the primary purpose of these entities is to generate mass sales for the affiliated producer by soliciting groups at a national or regional level and by providing leads to the affiliated agencies. The specialty marketing groups earn their revenue by receiving a commission from the insurer to cover profit and the costs of the marketing programs they operate. These affiliations may be available to a producer who is not representing an insurer with a network and who would otherwise be unable to take advantage of national mass marketing. However, if the programs are not competitive in a particular area, or if the sponsoring organization or the underwriting insurer is weak in the producer's territory, an affiliation with this sort of specialty group will be of little benefit to an agency. In contrast, if the programs sell, such an affiliation can greatly benefit the producer.

General Purpose Groups

General purpose groups are broader in scope than the affiliations that primarily market commercial group insurance products. The purpose of such organizations is to provide the affiliated agencies with a diverse package of resources, including educational opportunities, preferential treatment for affiliated agencies from certain insurers, a forum in which to exchange information with other agencies, and management assistance. These organizations feature meetings of affiliated agencies in which marketing and management information is exchanged. An annual fee paid by each affiliated agency supports the group's activities, and many of the meetings and seminars offered may be at an additional cost to the affiliated agency. General purpose groups try to attract top producing and servicing agencies so that the exchange of information is beneficial to those participating. An affiliated producer can learn much by meeting with producers from other areas of the country with similar problems and concerns. An example of such a group is the independent insurance agency distribution organization, Group 500.

Common Identity Groups

Common identity groups are established to give the participating firms national or international presence and resources. An organization like Assurex Global offers affiliated agencies facilities in major insurance centers throughout the U.S. and abroad. The primary emphasis of such a group is account servicing, and participants are likely to be large agencies that require reliable affiliates for local service on interstate or international accounts. Such groups may also participate in a common advertising program or otherwise identify themselves as affiliates. Current group members tend to be selective in choosing new affiliates so that they can be certain that the quality of the participating firms remains high. The costs of operating the network are paid by the participating firms via an annual service fee.

Evaluating Other Affiliations

Agencies and their producers have many opportunities to affiliate with various kinds of support organizations. Producers must determine whether any of these organizations can benefit their agencies. A producer considering an affiliation of any kind should talk not only to those who are offering the affiliation but also to some participants. It is also useful to find references who are not satisfied with the affiliation or who have rejected it so that both positive and negative information can be considered. In deciding on an affiliation, a producer should evaluate these factors:

- Services provided
- Personnel
- Exclusivity
- Fees
- Contract
- Financial strength

Services Provided

Any organization seeking to affiliate with insurance agencies offers a variety of services to prospects. Some of these services are attractive to producers considering affiliation, and others may not be useful and may even be harmful. A producer looking for a way to service national accounts from a single location is attracted to an affiliation that provides contacts across the United States. A producer who wants access to products to sell may be attracted to commercial mass marketing insurance programs, and a producer who needs management assistance might find some form of network desirable.

The producer should investigate each service carefully to learn exactly how it is going to be delivered to the agency. Selection of a service should be based more on services that are currently being provided than on those that are promised for some time in the future.

Personnel

Evaluating the available services is important, but evaluating who will be responsible for them is crucial. Services might seem to be outstanding, but the individuals behind the services ultimately determine the success of any affiliation. A producer who is considering affiliation must check references given by those in the support organization to be certain not only that the people are reliable but also that they are experienced insurance professionals.

Exclusivity

Many of the organizations with which an agency can affiliate are exclusive in one way or another. Often this exclusivity makes the organization attractive to a producer. It is important to determine how many other agencies in the immediate marketing area can join. It is also important to determine the legal nature of the exclusivity and the contract rights of an affiliated agency to a particular territory. Another factor is the reputation of those firms already participating in the program. An agency can derive prestige from the affiliation only if other participants meet the standards described by the sponsoring organization.

Fees

A major factor in determining whether to affiliate is the cost of the affiliation. Some of the options available to the producer cost little or nothing, whereas others can be expensive. Agency principals should question whether the services offered are worth the price being charged and whether the agency can afford them. Often, similar services may be available from other sources, so the producer considering an affiliation must try to unbundle the services offered and price them separately. All costs should be known to the agency in advance. Sometimes the prices quoted can be negotiated, so the producer should investigate this as well, especially in the case of new organizations that may be more willing to make a deal to obtain new business.

Contract

The agency considering an affiliation should look carefully at the contract to be signed between the agency and the sponsoring organization, if the association is going to be a formal one. The documents should be examined to determine the agency's responsibilities and to see what benefits to the agency are guaranteed by the contract. An attorney should review any agreement that the producer is considering.

Financial Strength

The larger the commitment the sponsoring organization undertakes, the more important are the financial resources to ensure delivery of the services. Producers considering affiliations should determine and be comfortable with the organization's financial strength and stability. The best way to determine this information is to talk to the top personnel about the organization's business philosophy, financial performance over time, and current financial status.

INSURANCE PRODUCERS AND REGULATION

Insurance producers have a responsibility to obey the laws and regulations that govern their business activities. Failure to meet this legal responsibility may cause loss of license and other penalties. The laws and regulations pertaining to insurance provide minimum standards of acceptable behavior with which agency personnel should comply.

Unlike regulation of other interstate businesses, regulation of insurance rests with the states rather than the federal government. This is largely the result of the McCarran-Ferguson Act (Public Law 15), a federal law passed in 1945.[3] In passing the act, the United States Congress expressed the belief that continued state regulation of insurance was in the public interest. Therefore, no act of Congress is to be "construed to invalidate, impair, and supersede any law enacted by any state for the purpose of regulating the business of insurance, or which imposes a fee or tax upon such businesses."[4] Federal laws apply to insurance only to the extent that state regulations do not apply.

Federal Regulations Affecting Insurance Producers

No federal legislation enacted since 1945 has attempted to specifically regulate the relationship between policyholders and privately owned insurers (including the Gramm-Leach-Bliley Act of 1999, which reaffirmed the McCarran-Ferguson Act). Nevertheless, many federal regulations of several federal agencies affect the daily activities of insurance producers.

Dodd-Frank Wall Street Reform and Consumer Protection Act

Title V—Insurance Subtitle A of the Dodd-Frank Wall Street Reform and Consumer Protection Act created the Federal Insurance Office within the Department of the Treasury. The office monitors the insurance industry for gaps in regulation and whether underserved communities have access to affordable insurance. Subtitle B State-Based Insurance Reform requires a state to participate in the national insurance producer database.

Securities and Exchange Commission (SEC)

The Securities and Exchange Commission (SEC) is a federal regulatory agency for the securities industry whose responsibility is to protect investors and maintain the integrity of the securities markets. Because of an exception in the securities laws, the SEC does not have regulatory authority over the sale of most life insurance. However, the Supreme Court has ruled, for regulatory purposes, that variable life insurance and variable annuities are "securities" rather than insurance policies. To sell these products legally, a producer must hold a federal securities license and abide by federal regulations. Property-casualty insurance does not have any investment features that would subject it to federal securities laws.

Federal Emergency Management Agency (FEMA)

The purpose of the Federal Emergency Management Agency (FEMA), a part of the Department of Homeland Security's Emergency Preparedness and Response Directorate, is to prepare the nation for all hazards that can potentially cause major loss of life and of property and to effectively manage federal response and recovery efforts after any national incident. FEMA also initiates mitigation activities, trains first responders, and manages the National Flood Insurance Program (NFIP) and the U.S. Fire Administration. In administering the NFIP, FEMA sets the insurance rates, coverage limits, and eligibility requirements for flood insurance. Any licensed producer may place insurance through the NFIP, either directly or indirectly, using private insurers as servicing companies.

Department of Transportation (DOT)

The Department of Transportation (DOT) is a federal department established to ensure a fast, safe, efficient, accessible, and convenient transportation system in the U.S. The department does not regulate insurance producers. However, DOT regulations affect insurance because they specify limits of insurance that commercial truckers must carry in different cargo and usage circumstances. The Motor Carrier Act of 1980 substantially increased the effect of these regulations on insurance sales. A producer who insures commercial vehicles must be aware of applicable DOT regulations and provide a trucker with all prescribed insurance.

Fair Credit Reporting Act

The Fair Credit Reporting Act of 1970 is a federal law enforced by the Federal Trade Commission. The law's purpose is to protect consumers from the disclosure of inaccurate and arbitrary personal information held by consumer reporting agencies and to establish procedures for reporting and correcting credit record mistakes.[5] The act requires an insurer to inform an insurance applicant in advance if it intends to order various consumer reports. In addition to credit and claim history, these reports may also contain information about an applicant's lifestyle, habits, personal character, and reputation. When an insurer acts based on information contained in these reports, the applicant has the right to ask the insurer which company provided the information. The consumer reporting company must then inform the applicant of its findings. The applicant can challenge the information. The applicant's version of the information must be added to the file by the reporting company and given to those who inquire about that individual.

Because insurance agencies and brokerages submit insurance applications, the producer may be responsible for providing appropriate notice to the applicant that various consumer reports may be obtained as part of the application process. Most insurance applications contain written disclosure notices and require the applicant to acknowledge the notice.

E&O Alert

Although insurance producers are subject to federal laws regarding consumer information, some states have their own fair credit reporting acts with more stringent disclosure requirements than the federal law. Producers must comply not only with federal law but also with state laws. Some consumer reporting companies have developed training courses for producers that detail consumer protection requirements imposed by state law and the Fair Credit Reporting Act.

[DA08162]

Gramm-Leach-Bliley Act

The Financial Services Modernization Act of 1999, also called the Gramm-Leach-Bliley Act, is a federal law that promotes affiliation and diversification in the nation's financial banks, insurers, and brokerages and protects consumers' personal financial information held by financial institutions.[6] The act allows banks, insurance agencies, and brokerages to have ownership interest in one another, a right that did not exist previously in all states. Additionally, the act requires all financial institutions, including insurance agencies, to establish policies about how to collect and disclose nonpublic personal financial information about customers.

Electronic Signatures in Global and National Commerce Act (ESIGN)

The Electronic Signatures in Global and National Commerce Act (ESIGN) of 2000 is a federal law designed to facilitate the use of electronic records and signatures in interstate and foreign commerce by ensuring the validity and legal effect of contracts entered into electronically.[7] ESIGN declares the validity of electronic signatures for interstate and international commerce (including insurance transactions), prohibits denial of the legal effect of certain electronic documents and transactions signed with an electronic signature, and clarifies the circumstances under which an electronic record satisfies any statute or regulation that mandates a record in writing.

USA Patriot Act

The USA Patriot Act of 2001, enacted after the September 11, 2001, terrorist attacks, makes it harder for terrorists, other criminal entities, and individuals to engage in money-laundering activities.[8] The law requires financial institutions to establish anti-money-laundering programs. However, property-casualty and health operations of insurers, insurance agents, and brokers are exempt from the Patriot Act's anti-money-laundering regulations. The reporting and compliance requirements apply to life insurers but not directly to life insurance agents. However, life insurers may integrate agents into their compliance programs.

Sarbanes-Oxley Act

The purpose of the Sarbanes-Oxley Act of 2002, officially called the Corporate and Auditing Accountability, Responsibility, and Transparency Act, was to introduce reforms to enhance corporate responsibility, enhance financial disclosures, and combat corporate and accounting fraud.[9] The act applies to companies listed on U.S. stock exchanges; companies otherwise obligated to file reports under the Securities and Exchange Act; and officers, employees, contractors, subcontractors, and agents of those companies. These categories include most insurers and a few large insurance agencies and brokerages. The act addresses accounting and financial reporting abuses by tightening internal accounting controls and holding company executives responsible for financial misdeeds. The act is also designed to reduce conflicts of interest between external audit firms and the companies they audit, as well as to increase the independence of board members.

CAN-SPAM Act

The CAN-SPAM Act of 2003 (Controlling the Assault of Non-Solicited Pornography and Marketing Act) addresses the problem of unsolicited commercial e-mail (spam). The act applies to "any electronic mail message whose primary purpose is to commercially advertise or promote a commercial product or service."[10] Such e-mail messages, unless exempt from the act, should include a notice that the message is an advertisement or solicitation, a notice of the opportunity to opt out of future commercial messages, and a valid physical postal address of the sender. The act exempts messages to a firm's customers that facilitate, complete, or confirm a commercial transaction. Insurance producers who have already established business with current customers and are electronically corresponding regarding insurance transactions or the general insurance relationship are exempt from the act. However, customer correspondence that is obviously an advertisement for a new product not previously discussed should comply with the act and include the opt-out notice.

Telemarketing and Consumer Fraud and Abuse Prevention Act and the Do Not Call Implementation Act

The Telemarketing and Consumer Fraud and Abuse Prevention Act of 1994 is the primary federal law governing telemarketers.[11] Its regulations include prohibiting repeated calls or prolonged conversation, limiting calls to between 8 am and 9 pm daily, and requiring telemarketers to reveal their identities and the purpose of the call.

Under authority granted to the Federal Trade Commission (FTC), the Telemarketing Sales Rule portion of the Telemarketing Consumer Fraud and Abuse Prevention Act was amended in 2002 to include national do-not-call regulations. The Do Not Call Implementation Act of 2003 authorizes the FTC to implement and enforce the do-not-call provisions of the Telemarketing Sales Rule and to impose fees on telemarketer violations to pay for the national do-not-call registry.

The FTC maintains a do-not-call registry in which consumers can enroll to indicate their unwillingness to accept unsolicited telemarketing calls. Businesses are prohibited from calling a consumer listed in the registry for the purpose of selling a product or service. Exceptions are made for established business relationships, political organizations, charities, not-for-profit organizations, entities conducting surveys, and bill collectors. The act also applies to cell phones and to residential, but not commercial, numbers. Many states have implemented separate do-not-call registries for consumers that may be subject to rules different from the federal rules. Insurance agencies that make cold calls to prospects should carefully research these federal and state laws. See the exhibit "Federal Laws That Affect Insurance Producers."

State Regulations Affecting Insurance Producers

Insurance activities in each state are regulated by a state insurance department. The names for the state regulatory agencies vary. In some states, the insurance regulatory unit is combined with the regulatory unit for another industry, such as banking. In this text, state regulating agencies are called insurance departments, and the individuals who head those departments are called commissioners.

Insurers and insurance producers are often subject to state regulatory constraints. Five areas of state regulation that directly affect producers are:

1. Licensing laws
2. Unfair trade practices acts
3. Unfair claims settlement practices acts
4. Regulations governing the handling of premiums
5. Regulations governing dealing with suitable insurers

Licensing Laws

Producers must be licensed in each state in which they transact business. Those who operate without a license are subject to civil and, possibly, criminal penalties. The majority of states have adopted the NAIC's Producer Licensing Model Act. In doing so, they have replaced the license

Federal Laws That Affect Insurance Producers

Dodd-Frank Wall Street Reform and Consumer Protection Act

Created the Federal Insurance Office and requires states to participate in the national insurance producer database

McCarran-Ferguson Act (Public Law 15)

Establishes that insurance regulation rests with the states rather than the federal government

Fair Credit Reporting Act

Protects consumers from the disclosure of inaccurate and arbitrary personal information held by consumer reporting agencies and establishes procedures for reporting and correcting credit record mistakes; enforced by the Federal Trade Commission

Financial Services Modernization Act of 1999/Gramm-Leach-Bliley Act

Promotes affiliation and diversification in the nation's financial banks, insurers, and brokerage firms and includes privacy requirements that protect consumers' personal financial information held by financial institutions

Electronic Signatures in Global and National Commerce Act (ESIGN)

Facilitates the use of electronic records and signatures in interstate and foreign commerce by ensuring the validity and legal effect of contracts entered into electronically

USA Patriot Act

Makes it harder for terrorists, other criminal entities, and individuals to engage in money-laundering activities

Sarbanes-Oxley Act

Criminalizes many corporate acts, including accounting abuses, that were previously relegated to various regulatory authorities

CAN-SPAM Act

Addresses the problem of unsolicited commercial e-mail (spam)

[DA08163]

classifications of agent and broker with the single license classification of producer. Some states issue separate agent, broker, and solicitor licenses; others issue only agents' licenses, in which case brokers become agents of the particular insurer involved in each transaction. Still other states issue combined agent/broker licenses, and the status of the transactor is determined by an agency agreement. Most states require separate licenses for insurance agencies that operate as corporations, partnerships, or other legal entities.

All states require producers to pass an examination sponsored by the insurance department that is administered either by the department or by an independent testing service. States differ in the difficulty of their exams and the number of exams an applicant must pass to sell particular lines of insurance. Some states require applicants to complete some classroom training

E&O Alert

The definition of "transact" varies by state. However, most jurisdictions require a license to conduct the following activities:

- Solicit applications for insurance

- Negotiate before a contract of insurance is executed

- Execute a contract of insurance

- Transact any insurance matters subsequent to executing the original contract

Agencies have been fined for failing to license producers and other agency support personnel who are considered to "transact" business, as defined by the state's insurance code.

[DA08164]

before taking the license examination. Some states waive the exam for applicants who take an exam similar to the department exam after completing an approved course or who hold certain professional insurance designations. Some states have reciprocal agreements whereby that state's exam is waived for producers who have met the requirements in other states. However, those states that have implemented the PLMA have standards for who should be licensed, license classifications, lines of authority, and license applications.

Licenses generally have a term of one or two years but are usually renewed with payment of a fee. Most states, however, have introduced mandatory continuing education or reexamination requirements that producers must satisfy to renew their licenses. In 1978, the NAIC adopted a model regulation establishing continuing education requirements, but states requiring continuing education set their own standards.

Countersignature laws
Laws that require all policies covering subjects of insurance within a state to be signed by a resident producer licensed in that state.

All but a few states have eliminated their **countersignature laws**, which required all policies covering subjects of insurance within a state to be signed by a resident producer licensed in that state.

Management Tip—Although required continuing education is a controversial issue—due, in part, to the time and expense involved in relation to the perceived benefit—producers who want to be viewed as professionals should not rely on the state to determine the proper level of training and education. Continuing, goal-oriented professional development should be part of every agency employee's job and is more important than ever in today's competitive environment.

Provisions of countersignature laws may require that the resident producer be paid some fraction (usually 25 percent to 50 percent) of the total commission. These laws are facing strong challenges and are being eliminated because some regulators believe they are archaic and unnecessary, and some courts believe them to be unconstitutional restrictions on interstate commerce.

Specific regulations affecting producer licensing vary by state. This text does not describe all these regulations. Licensed producers should know the applicable licensing regulations affecting their business operations.

> **E&O Alert**
>
> Every agency and brokerage should have a current copy of the state insurance code or know where to find it on the Internet. This code is an important reference tool for determining acceptable actions and agency procedures. Many state insurance departments have Web sites where producers can access the current insurance code and download both the text of the law and any applicable regulations.

[DA08165]

Unfair Trade Practices Act

Other state regulations that directly affect producers involve unfair trade practices. **Unfair trade practices** are methods of competition or advertising or procedures that tend to deprive the public of information needed to make informed insurance decisions. Individuals engaging in any unfair trade practices may be subject to cease and desist orders, loss of licenses, or heavy fines.

The NAIC has developed a model act relating to unfair trade practices in the business of insurance. All states have laws based on the Model Act. The exhibit defines unfair trade practices common to the NAIC Model Act and many state laws. Although states vary in how they address these practices, the Model Act represents a consensus regarding practices in which producers should not engage and for which they may incur penalties. All producers transacting insurance in a particular state must carefully examine the provisions of that state's unfair trade practices act. See the exhibit "Common Unfair Trade Practices."

Unfair trade practices
Methods of competition or advertising or procedures that tend to deprive the public of information necessary to make informed insurance decisions.

Common Unfair Trade Practices

Misrepresentation and/or False Advertising—An insurer's written or oral statement that does not accurately describe an insurance policy's coverage or benefits.

Defamation—A false, malicious, or abusive written or oral communication that harms another's reputation or character.

Boycott, Coercion, or Intimidation—The act of compelling an insurance consumer to purchase from a particular producer or insurer.

Twisting—The unethical act of persuading a policyholder to cancel or replace a policy solely to sell another policy, without regard to possible negative consequences to the policyholder.

Rebating—The act of providing the buyer of an insurance policy a portion of the amount of the policy premium he or she paid (or the producers' commission) or anything of significant tangible value in return for purchasing the policy (permitted in some states, such as California and Florida under certain conditions).

[DA08166]

Unfair Claims Settlement Practices Acts

Another kind of regulation that directly affects producers is unfair claims settlement practices regulation. Both the NAIC Model Act and state unfair trade practices acts contain a separate section dealing with unfair claim settlement practices, and most states have adopted versions of them. The purpose of these laws is to protect insureds and claimants during the claim filing, investigation, and settlement process. Although many of these laws concern insurers and their claim representatives, they also affect insurance producers. Most unfair claims practices regulations set specific time frames for communicating with claimants and policyholders. These time frames are binding on producers as well as on insurers. Improperly handling claims can expose the agency to regulatory penalties as well as to errors and omissions claims. The exhibit summarizes the unfair claims settlement practices to which state laws commonly apply. See the exhibit "Common Unfair Claims Settlement Practices."

Common Unfair Claims Settlement Practices

- Knowingly misrepresenting policy provisions to a claimant or insured at the time of the claim

- Failing to promptly acknowledge pertinent communications about a claim

- Failing to adopt and use reasonable standards for settling claims

- Attempting to settle claims late and/or unfairly when the insurer's liability has become reasonably clear

- Failing to affirm or deny coverage of a claim within a reasonable period after receiving a proof of loss statement

- Attempting to settle a claim for less than could be reasonably expected, according to public advertising material

- Failing to offer a reasonable and accurate explanation for denying a claim

- Compelling policyholders to file suit to recover amounts due them by offering them substantially less than the amounts that could be recovered by litigation

- Refusing to pay claims while conducting a reasonable investigation based on all available information

- Engaging in activities that result in a disproportionate number of complaints against the insurer received by the state insurance departments

- Failing to provide necessary claim forms promptly, including explanations about how to use the forms effectively

[DA08167]

Handling Premiums

Premium handling regulations also directly affect producers. A producer collects insurance premiums on the insurer's behalf and acts as the insurer's fiduciary for these premiums. In many states, the premiums must be kept in a separate trust account and must not be commingled with other personal or business funds. Failure to comply with this requirement can subject the producer to civil and criminal penalties, including fines, loss of license, and imprisonment.

E&O Alert

Although most of the issues addressed by claims settlement practices acts involve insurers rather than producers, any action or inaction on the producer's part that impairs the insurer's ability to handle a claim may cause an E&O loss for the agency or brokerage. Consider these real-life scenarios: a producer was found guilty on federal charges after a routine audit by the department of insurance revealed that premiums were being diverted for the producer's personal use. In addition to sanctions by the department, the producer was sentenced to a federal prison term. In another incident, a producer who collected premiums from customers but failed to remit them to the insurer had his license revoked. The misappropriation of premiums and breach of the agent's fiduciary duty will invariably cause severe penalties as well as loss of customers and damaged business reputation.

[DA08168]

Dealing With Suitable Insurers

State regulations governing relations with suitable insurers also directly affect producers. The purpose of these regulations is to prohibit producers from writing insurance with insurers not licensed or admitted to do business in the state, unless the producers have special licenses to do so, or unless they broker the insurance through an individual or entity that is licensed. Producers involved in an insurance transaction without complying with this licensing requirement can be held personally liable and can also lose their licenses.

E&O Alert

All states have regulations regarding the authority of insurers to operate in that state. In some states, producers placing business with approved, or "admitted," insurers or with authorized unapproved, or "nonadmitted," insurers are relieved of legal liability to their customers if the insurer subsequently becomes insolvent. This regulation is based on the premise that the insurance department is responsible for determining the financial stability of the insurer before allowing it to do business in the state. However, if a producer places business with an unauthorized insurer, the insurer's insolvency could prompt an E&O claim against the producer. Producers should be aware of their states' regulations regarding admitted and nonadmitted insurers. Producers should use due diligence before recommending an insurer to a customer. One definition of due diligence is the diligence an individual can reasonably expect to exercise in discharging a duty or an obligation and the diligence that, in turn, can reasonably be expected from that individual.

In an insurance context, a producer's responsibility in using due diligence includes determining the insurer's legal status, analyzing the insurer's financial ability to provide the purchased coverage, and evaluating the insurer's suitability for the customer and the customer's loss exposures. Failure to use due diligence could expose a producer to an E&O claim.

[DA08169]

SUMMARY

Principals and agents owe different obligations to each other. An agent's duties to a principal include loyalty, obedience, reasonable care, accounting, and information. The principal has four remedies for an agent's default or wrongdoing. The principal can sue to require the agent to transfer improperly held property to the principal; sue for the value of the benefit the agent received; sue for breach of agency contract; or sue in tort for harm done.

A principal has the duty to provide the agent with an agreed-on period of employment, compensation, reimbursement for expenses, and indemnity for losses. If the principal breaches any of these duties, the agent can sue for compensation, indemnity, or reimbursement; alternatively, the agent can retain possession of the principal's goods until the principal has paid any amounts due.

The agency-principal relationship in insurance varies based on the scope of duties of agents and brokers and the authority of agents. Authority is the legal power of the agent arising from the agency relationship. An agent's power to bind the principal can be determined to be express authority, implied authority, or apparent authority.

In addition to agency creation by contract, an agency can be created by ratification when the principal accepts a transaction that exceeds an agent's express or implied authority. An agent's status as an independent contractor transfers liability loss exposures for the independent contractor's actions from the insurer to the independent contractor. Agents may sometimes act for an undisclosed or partially disclosed principal or for a nonexistent principal. In each of the cases, laws to protect the public's welfare may result in greater liability exposure for an agent than liability in cases involving a completely disclosed principal.

Compliance with state licensing laws has been a source of frustration and expense for producers due to lack of uniformity. Recently, however, the NIPR, with its PDB electronic database and NIPR Gateway communication network, has made progress in addressing producers' concerns. Regarding the licensing of claim representatives and insurance consultants, a lack of uniformity remains, as some states require them to be licensed and others do not.

An insurance agency-insurance company contract typically contains seven major sections and a separate commissions and/or contingent commission agreement schedule section that varies among agencies. The seven major sections of an insurance agency contract are:

1. Term of agreement/termination
2. Rehabilitation
3. Ownership of expirations
4. Payment procedures
5. Indemnification
6. Contract amendments
7. Miscellaneous provisions

Principals may choose from one of three legal forms when creating an insurance agency:

- Sole proprietorship, an organization owned by a single individual who assumes all personal and tax liability for the business
- Partnership, a voluntary association of two or more persons who are co-owners of a business and who agree to share in its profits and/or losses
- Corporation, a business enterprise that is an independent legal entity, owned by its owners, who are called stockholders, and managed by a board of directors elected by the stockholders

An insurer's selection of the legal form should be made in partnership with legal and tax experts.

Insurance agencies form operating affiliations to reach additional customers and prospects, to take advantage of new marketing opportunities, and to realize economies of scale. Types of operating affiliations include these:

- Independent agency networks
- Insurance company affiliations
- Specialty marketing groups
- General purpose groups
- Common identity groups

Agencies should carefully evaluate each type of independent agency network and the benefits they offer before making a decision. This evaluation should consider issues such as services provided, personnel, exclusivity, fees, contracts, and financial strength.

Insurance producers are subject primarily to state regulation. However, the federal regulations that do affect agents originate from the Securities and Exchange Commission; the Federal Emergency Management Agency; the Department of Transportation; the Federal Trade Commission, which enforces the Fair Credit Reporting Act; the Gramm-Leach-Bliley Act; the Electronic Signatures in Global and National Commerce Act (ESIGN); the USA Patriot Act; the Sarbanes-Oxley Act; The CAN-SPAM Act; the Telemarketing and Consumer Fraud and Abuse Act; and the Do Not Call Implementation Act. Principal areas of state regulation affecting producers include licensing, unfair trade practices, the handling of premiums, and choice of insurers.

ASSIGNMENT NOTES

1. Bertram Harnett Responsibilities of Insurance Agents and Brokers, vol. I (Newark, N.J.: Matthew Bender & Company, 2004), p. 2–202.3

2. Independent Insurance Agents and Brokers of America, Independent Agent's Guide to Agency-Company Agreements (Alexandria, Va.: IIABA, 1993). Adaptation of updated version used with permission of IIABA Contracts Committee and Independent Insurance Agents of Texas, 2002, www.iiat.org (accessed September 6, 2004).

3. 15 U.S.C. § 1011–1015.

4. 15 U.S.C. § 1011 et seq.

5. 15 U.S.C. § 1681.

6. 15 U.S.C. § 6801–6809 et seq.

7. 15 U.S.C. § 7001.

8. Public Law 107-56 [H.R. 3162].

9. 18 U.S.C. § 1514A.

10. U.S. S877 (2003).

11. 15 U.S.C. §§ 1601–1608.

Direct Your Learning ▶▶

2

Organizational Management

Educational Objectives

After learning the content of this assignment, you should be able to:

▷ Describe the four major functions of management including these specific aspects of planning:

- Characteristics of a plan
- Types of plans
- Steps in the planning process

▷ Describe these specific aspects of the organizing function of management:

- Determining forms of organizational structure
- Developing organizational position descriptions
- Evaluating staffing needs

▷ Explain how managers lead employees by motivating, delegating, and managing conflict.

▷ Describe these specific aspects of the controlling function of management:

- The four steps in the control process
- The factors managers should consider when evaluating employee performance

Organizational Management

ORGANIZATIONAL MANAGEMENT AND PLANNING

Management is a set of functions that enable an organization to achieve its goals efficiently and effectively.

The four functions of **management** are described as:

1. Planning—identifying and selecting organizational goals and the means to best achieve those goals
2. Organizing—establishing task and authority relationships that allow people to work together to achieve organizational goals
3. Leading—motivating, coordinating, and energizing individuals and groups to work together to achieve organizational goals
4. Controlling—establishing accurate measuring and monitoring systems to evaluate how well the organization is achieving its goals

Management
The set of functions, including planning, organizing, leading, and controlling resources, that enable organizations to achieve their goals efficiently and effectively.

Planning

Planning helps insurance agency owners and managers decide what results they want to achieve. Part of effective planning includes identifying the organization's needed resources and determining the organization's relationship to its external environment.

Careful planning is just as important for small organizations as it is for large organizations because all organizations need to identify specific courses of action if they wish to achieve desired results. Careful planning also can reduce costs and increase profits because it focuses on what is most important in order for an organization to achieve its goals and on how to allocate resources to those goals.

Planning provides a means for the organization to progress from where it is to where it wants to be. This section discusses characteristics of efficient and effective plans, types of plans, and the planning process.

Plan Characteristics

Plans are written records documenting the organization's mission, goals, strategies, objectives, budgets, policies, and procedures. The purpose of a plan is to minimize the degree to which an organization is surprised by unforeseen, costly events.

Plans that are developed by involving the entire organization are generally more effective than plans that are developed solely by senior management. An effective and efficient plan must have these four characteristics:

1. *Unity.* Only one centralized guiding plan should be put into operation at a time to achieve the organization's mission and goals. Putting multiple plans into operation may cause confusion and can be counter to the organization's mission and goals.

2. *Continuity.* The organization's manager can build on previous plans and continually modify current plans (corporate, business, and functional) so they fit into a single organizational framework.

3. *Accuracy.* Managers should gather and use all available relevant information in the planning process, recognizing that inaccuracy can result from incompleteness.

4. *Flexibility.* Managers should be able to modify the plan when changes are necessary. Unless it is flexible, the plan cannot respond to the dynamic requirements of a changing environment.

Plan Types

Large organizations have three major types of plans for different organizational levels. Together, they should be consistent and designed to carry out the organization's goals. The three types of plans are:

Corporate plan

A plan that contains senior management's decisions relating to the organization's corporate goals.

*   **Corporate plans** are strategic—that is, the plan sets the overall course and direction for the organization. Strategic goals are long-term, usually taking two to four years to accomplish. The organizational goals and corporate-level strategy should support the corporate mission. Generally, the corporate mission is a broad, concise statement of the primary corporate purpose, products, services, and markets, and it is designed to be long-standing. The mission, goals, and strategy expressed in a corporate plan can often provide a preliminary indication of the markets in which an organization intends to compete. For example, one organization's goal as stated in its corporate plan is to be among the top five in private passenger auto market share in every state in which it competes.

Business plan (divisional plan)

A plan that contains divisional managers' decisions about the division's goals and how the division will support the organization's corporate goals.

*   **Business (divisional) plans** are created by each manager at the business level. These plans not only support the corporate goals but also reflect the strengths, weaknesses, opportunities, and threats present in the business-level environment. For example, if a national insurance broker's corporate goal is to expand its private passenger auto market by 20 percent over the coming year, a branch agency's business-level plan may include a goal to

purchase its next largest competitor, which specializes in monoline auto coverages.

- **Functional plans** are made at the department or similar unit level. A function is a specialized group in which individuals have similar skills or use the same resources to accomplish tasks. Examples of functions include marketing, accounting, manufacturing, and research and development. Assume a corporate plan includes the goal to attain an earnings growth of 10 percent. A business plan goal in support of this corporate goal may be to increase cash flow from operations by 15 percent. A functional plan goal made by the accounting manager, in support of the business and corporate goals, may be to ensure that 90 percent of aged accounts receivable are collected within a specified period.

Functional plan

A plan that contains managers' decisions about the functional unit's goals and how the functional unit will support the division's and the organization's corporate goals.

Planning Process

Plans are guides to action. The planning process includes these seven steps:

- Develop a mission statement
- Develop goals
- Develop strategies
- Develop objectives
- Develop budgets
- Establish policies and procedures
- Monitor the plan

The planning process allows an organization to set the direction for the other functions of management: organizing, leading, and controlling.

Develop a Mission Statement

The first step in the planning process is to develop a mission statement. This step may not be required every time if the mission statement has already been developed. The mission statement should be broadly stated and needs-based—that is, focused on the desire to meet the needs of current and potential customers. However, even if broadly stated, the mission may need to be reevaluated in light of major corporate changes, such as when an organization shifts its marketing focus. For example, if a regional agency merges with a competitor, making it national in scope, a corporate mission statement that partially reads, "To serve the insurance needs of the Northeast region..." would need to be revised to reflect the agency's broadened sales and marketing capability.

Consider these examples of mission statements. They differ in scope, yet all meet the criteria of properly constructed mission statements:

- "To provide risk management services to my community" (broad statement)
- "To find those people or organizations I can serve within the restrictions of my agency contract" (narrower statement made by an agent of a direct writer)
- "To serve the financial services needs of the Philadelphia community" (statement broad in service and narrow in geographic area)

Sometimes organizations develop a vision statement to accompany the mission statement. A vision statement is intended to be an inspiring and positive description of what the organization aspires to and usually includes the values that guide the organization.

Develop Goals

The second step in the planning process is to develop goals. Goals are the final desired results for the planning period, whether strategic (long term) or short term. To illustrate, the following is an example of a strategic goal: "Our agency will generate $1 million in new commission income within the next three years." An example of a short-term goal is: "Our agency will decrease the amount of outstanding accounts receivable by 50 percent within the next six months."

Both goals and objectives have certain characteristics. To be effective, each goal or objective should possess five "SMART" characteristics:

- Specific
- Measurable
- Achievable
- Relevant
- Time bound

Managers must have a specific result in mind when setting goals. A production goal "to increase production" does little to indicate what results are expected other than to produce more. However, a stated goal to sell policies generating $10,000 in commission per month clearly shows the specific results.

Measurable means that at the end of the planning period the goal can be said either to have or to have not been accomplished. The preceding production goal is stated in specific terms and is measurable in dollars. The goal could also be stated in percentage terms or in any other appropriate unit of measure.

Goals also must be achievable. Forecasting helps to determine whether goals are achievable. For example, assume an insurance agency wants to have a production goal. Forecasts that project variables such as market size, growth trends, and expenses can help an agency set realistic production goals.

Forecasts can be made for both internal and external areas of the organization. Internal forecasts, such as annual employee turnover forecasts, are easier to develop. However, external forecasts are equally important. For external goal-setting, forecasts are required in such areas as the customer's demographic characteristics, the nature of the competition, economic conditions, regulatory practices, and insurance market availability.

Goals must also be relevant. They should align with and support the organization's mission and improve organizational value. For example, a property-casualty insurance agency's goal to "increase annual sales of financial services-related products by 20 percent" supports the agency's recently revised mission statement: "To provide premier insurance, risk management, and financial services products to our regional community."

Finally, managers must ensure that goals are time bound—that is, specific dates and times for completion are given, as well as milestones, if appropriate. Effective goals have fixed deadlines. Individuals are better able to focus on attaining goals when committed to deadlines. For instance, "I will complete my AAI designation someday," is not a time-bound goal. However, "I will complete my AAI designation within two years of my start date," is an example of a time-bound goal.

Develop Strategies

The third step in the planning process is to develop strategies. Strategies indicate how organizations plan to accomplish their missions and achieve their goals. Strategies are the series of decisions that form the foundation of organizational planning, and they should be shared throughout an organization to gain feedback and to coordinate activities. Strategy formulation relies on the internal and external forecasts completed during the organization's goal setting process.

Like plans themselves, strategies can be corporate, business, or functional. For example, an agency principal with the goal to "increase the agency's overall annual premium volume by 50 percent" may accomplish this goal by implementing a corporate strategy of merging with a small, local competitor.

Develop Objectives

The fourth step in the planning process is to develop objectives. Objectives are the milestones or intermediate steps required to achieve goals. Objectives always support a goal, and typically each goal has multiple objectives. Goals and objectives share the same SMART characteristics.

For example, for the previously stated goal, "Our agency will generate $1 million in new commission income within the next three years," supporting objectives could include:

- Design a sales campaign and a compensation plan by the end of the first quarter that motivates producers to generate enough business to qualify for bonuses or prizes
- Design an account upgrade campaign for current customers by the end of the second quarter

These illustrated objectives support one strategic goal for an agency. Each goal dictates a set of related objectives.

Develop Budgets

The fifth step in the planning process is to develop budgets. A budget is a written estimate of operating revenues and expenses for a future period. Budgets are usually expressed in units of money but can also be expressed in terms of other resources, such as time. Senior management determines what financial resources the organization will allocate to projects based on information provided by business units.

Budgets are integral parts of all types of plans. They enable management to assign numbers to the goals for the planning period and create a means of measuring progress toward those goals. A budget must be written and realistic, and it must include senior management's vision and line managers' operating expertise. Two types of budgets are operational budgets and capital budgets. Types of operational budgets include sales budgets, expense budgets, and cash budgets.

Managers develop budgets by projecting long-term figures (over one to three years) or short-term figures (up to one year). Budgeting should be more detailed in the short term than in the long term. The first year's budget should include monthly projections; the second year projections could include quarterly projections; and the subsequent years' budgets could include annual projections. As the first year nears its end, the second year's budget should be converted from quarterly to monthly, and so on. The short-term operating budgets are the sales budget, the expense budget, and the cash budget. Capital budgets, although closely linked to operating budgets, require a longer planning horizon than the one-year operating budgets.

When planning for growth, an agency should forecast sales for the next three years. However, for monitoring and control, the sales budget should be short-term—quarterly or even monthly. By checking sales levels against the budget, the organization can determine whether it is ahead of or behind planned production goals.

Every major expense category should be itemized in another short-term budget, the expense budget. The budget should project when expenses will be incurred and paid. For example, if an organization anticipates purchasing a large quantity of office supplies in June, the budget should indicate that a cash payment expense will be incurred in June. But if the expense will not be paid until August 1, then the budget should project an August 1 cash payment expense. Expense budgets can be a highly accurate way to calculate the amount of funds needed and when they will be needed, making this part of the budget important in determining the cash budget.

The short-term sales and expense budgets are among the items used to create the cash budget. The cash budget can reveal when excess cash will be available for short-term investment or when a loan will be needed to cover a period during which expenses paid exceed cash available. The cash budget helps the organization determine whether it will have enough cash or liquid assets on hand to meet its financial requirements in any situation at any given time.

The cash budget is based on the simple concept that the cash available minus the cash needed equals the cash balance. The cash available is determined by starting with the balance in last month's bank account and adding to this balance the cash receipts from previous months' bills to be collected. Also added are any liquidated investments, expected contingent commissions, or any other item that would produce cash.

Capital budgeting is the process of planning expenditures on assets whose returns are expected to extend beyond one year. Office renovations and the purchase of furnishings are examples of capital expenditures. Capital budgeting also includes long-term investment of excess cash. Organizations that have the excess cash required for such investments must evaluate the long-term risks as well as the returns on those investments.

Management Tip—When the budget has been established, alternative plans should also be developed to handle unanticipated results, such as a sudden, unforeseen increase in expenses or a change in market conditions. Management should investigate such results immediately. When the budget must be revised, deciding on alternative plans is easier if such plans have been identified as part of the initial budgeting process.

Establish Policies and Procedures

The sixth step in the planning process is to establish policies and procedures. Policies are guidelines for making decisions and performing activities. They may be stated narrowly or broadly. For example, a policy concerning producer time spent inside an agency may state: "Each producer will determine the appropriate amount of time to spend in the office for administrative and other nonselling activities. Management encourages producers to delegate as many of these activities as possible." This is an example of a broadly stated policy. At the other extreme is this narrowly stated policy on overdue accounts: "Any account overdue by thirty days will be canceled by the forty-fifth day, and notice of cancellation will be forwarded to the insured by registered mail. Any deviation from this policy must be approved by management."

A procedure is an established series of steps or instructions for performing normal and recurring activities. Procedures are an important part of the planning process because they can help the agency monitor and control both time and money. Procedures are usually established by employees at the functional level.

Procedures are useful as a guide not only to employees overall, but also to newly hired employees and to employees new to a position within the agency. Procedures clearly describe what needs to be done, in what order, and within what time frame (if applicable). This information enables employees to focus on identified goals and to have a course of action to follow to help reach those goals.

E&O Alert

Procedures also help prevent E&O claims because they can eliminate many of the mistakes that can occur if no clear procedures exist. Agency planning should involve designing procedures with this benefit in mind.

[DA08085]

Monitor the Plan

The seventh step in the planning process is to monitor the plan to evaluate its results and allow for any necessary corrections. Monitoring should be regular and timely, and it should be highly organized and formalized. Organizations typically use **management by exception**, that is, they monitor plans and may respond to results that differ from standards and/or parameters defined in the organization's goals and objectives. By monitoring only results that fall outside the goals and objectives, managers save time they would otherwise spend monitoring the results that meet or exceed the goals and objectives.

Management by exception

A management concept wherein management monitors plans and may respond to results that differ from standards and/ or parameters defined by the organization's goals and objectives.

The expected results of a plan are stated in clear, precise, and measurable terms. The organization's managers must evaluate and report actual results in relation to the plan's expected results. Regular progress reports should be required of and distributed to all personnel. These reports do not have to be elaborate, but they do have to be accurate. Progress reports promote discipline and focus on achievement, both of which are crucial to the timely and successful achievement of goals and objectives.

ORGANIZATIONAL MANAGEMENT AND ORGANIZING

Organizing is a fundamental management function that involves performing various activities that enable people to work together effectively to achieve the organization's goals and objectives. These activities include:

- Establishing the organizational structure, including defining relationships and designating who has authority and responsibility for various activities
- Creating a position description for each position in the organizational structure
- Establishing job qualifications for the person who fills each position
- Hiring the right number of people with the skills necessary to achieve the organization's goals and objectives

Organizations are composed of individuals who typically work in separate departments, business units, or other distinct organizational structures. Organizing and staffing these units and hiring the individuals in the organization are all part of a manager's responsibilities.

Structure

An organizational structure indicates who has authority and responsibility for what activities. Because a faulty structure can impair the organization's performance and hinder the achievement of its goals and objectives, organizational structures must be carefully planned and periodically reviewed.

One of the most common organizational problems is the failure to clarify organizational relationships. People need to know who is responsible for what and how authority and responsibility are delineated. Additionally, enough authority must be delegated to allow people to perform their designated responsibilities. Managers who hold employees responsible for activities over which they have no control create unworkable structures and often contribute to morale problems. Senior managers must be willing to delegate the authority necessary for people to handle their designated jobs effectively.

These three basic forms of organizational structure are based on delegated authority and responsibilities:

- Line
- Functional
- Line and staff

Line Organization

A **line organization** is likely to be the type adopted by a small insurance agency. Under this organizational structure, the principal (agency owner) assigns tasks directly to the office personnel and is ultimately responsible

Line organization
An organization that has a vertical structure in which authority flows from the top of the structure to the bottom and responsibility for delegated tasks flows in reverse.

for what the office personnel do. A simple line organization is shown in the exhibit. See the exhibit "Simple Line Organization."

Simple Line Organization

[DA08090]

Delegating internal activities works only if delegation is complete. An owner who fails to give the office manager sufficient authority to accomplish tasks may end up spending too much production time on management matters.

The advantage of a line organization is simplicity. This structure clearly indicates to employees who their managers are and who has organizational responsibility. A line organization structure can also help managers respond quickly to customer service issues. Line organizations are efficient for small businesses.

A disadvantage of line organizations is that they are based on the presumption that the firm's owners are competent in all phases of the business. The owners must deal with personnel, administrative office work, customer service, marketing, financial services, planning, and research. An owner who is inexperienced or untrained in any of these areas may overlook or ignore those areas to the detriment of the organization's profitability. In a small organization, the owner can cope with many decisions, but, as the organization grows, decisions become more difficult without specialists' help.

Perhaps the greatest disadvantage of a line organization is the possibility that the owner will be unable or unwilling to stop being involved in activities that are better performed by others. Often, when the business and the owner mature together, the owner has difficulty sharing authority.

Functional Organization

Functional organization

An organization in which the owner retains line authority but can staff each function with an expert in each respective area.

A **functional organization** can capitalize on the strengths of the line organization structure while minimizing some of its weaknesses. All experts within the organization have employees who report to them, lengthening the line of the organizational structure. The exhibit illustrates a functional organization in which expert function supervisors report to the owner, who retains line authority over staff. See the exhibit "Simple Functional (Nonline) Organization."

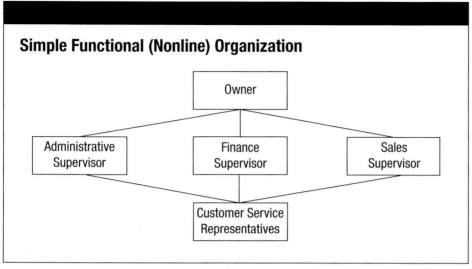

Simple Functional (Nonline) Organization

[DA08091]

The greatest advantage of functional organizations is that they are built around experts in each field. With specialized training in particular areas, these experts are better equipped to solve the problems in their functional areas than are line executives.

The effectiveness of this organizational structure depends on the behavior of the participants. If good communication and negotiations occur among the functions, functional expertise within the organization can improve productivity. New employees can also receive specialized training much more effectively in a functional organization than in a line organization.

A disadvantage of the functional organizational structure is that authority is divided, and this may create problems if an employee must report to more than one person. Having more than one boss can be frustrating and can cause confusion, particularly when the functional specialists disagree. The divided authority and responsibility of the functional structure can also delay action on decisions and result in compromise before a decision can be reached.

Line and Staff Organization

The functional organizational structure generally relies on employees who are experts in specific fields, whereas the line organizational structure tends to employ individuals with general skills who can contribute in many different areas. The **line and staff organization** is a combination of these two structures and is the most common structure used in mid-size and large insurance agencies.

The meshing of elements of line and staff organizations enables plans to be executed effectively by line staff with definite authority and responsibility. The staff specialists support the line functions, which are paramount. When their expertise is needed, the staff specialists can advise line staff. They serve in an advisory capacity with no line authority.

Line and staff organization

An organization that combines certain features of the line organization (which develops employees' general skills) and of the functional organization (which develops experts in specific fields).

The exhibit presents an example of an insurance agency organized on a line and staff basis, showing relationships among various positions. The line authority and responsibilities are shown by solid lines. For example, the training and sales managers receive line authority from and are responsible to the principal. However, the training manager advises only the office and sales managers. Therefore, the training function is viewed as staff by the office and sales managers. This agency is functionally organized because different people with specialized expertise are responsible for the functions of office administration (office manager), training (training manager), and sales (sales manager). The principal maintains simple line authority through a functional division of authority. See the exhibit "Hypothetical Line and Staff Organization."

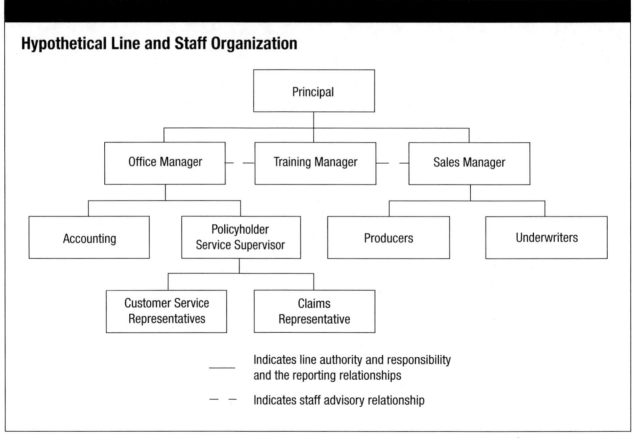

Hypothetical Line and Staff Organization

[DA08092]

Typically, a line and staff organization takes advantage of the strengths of both the line and functional structures. Each employee reports to only one person because authority and responsibility are fixed. If assistance is needed, specialists can be called on for help through the line executives. Line executives are not required to take the recommendations of staff, but they can benefit from their advice.

Accountability can be more defined and coordination can be improved in a line and staff organization as compared with limited functional organization structures. Additionally, inexperienced personnel can be trained in both line and staff areas.

The line and staff organizational structure presents a few disadvantages. At times, staff people attempt to assume line authority because they want to see their ideas implemented. Conversely, because line people can override the ideas of the staff, ideas that improve effectiveness and efficiency may not be implemented. Also, a line and staff organizational structure may not be possible for small organizations simply because they have an insufficient number of employees.

Management Tip—Although management experts have suggested various organizational concepts (power teams, pods, and so on) as alternatives to current structures, managers should understand that, in practice, these concepts are often simply different versions of a line and staff organization.

Position Descriptions

Once the organizational structure is in place, position descriptions for each job within the organization must be developed. Position descriptions are written summaries of particular jobs in an organization. Each "box" in an organizational chart should have a written position description. A position description states this:

- Position in the organization—The exhibit shows a position description for a commercial insurance producer. The top portion indicates where the position falls in the organization's hierarchy. The title of the job generally appears first, followed by the reporting relationship and then by the department in which the position is located. All this information naturally flows from the organizational structure.

- Overall responsibilities—The position's overall responsibilities and general activities are summarized in a one- or two-sentence paragraph. A more detailed description of responsibilities follows in a section about specific responsibilities.

- Specific responsibilities—The specific responsibilities are the heart of the position description. Employees should clearly know their job responsibilities and the basis on which their success or failure on the job will be measured. For the manager charged with developing a position description, the specific responsibilities section is important for two reasons. First, the manager establishes the performance expectations used to evaluate employees. Second, the specific responsibilities are important in determining the position qualifications. More information about this appears in the next section on position qualifications.

- Nature and scope—The nature and scope section of the position description shows how the position fits within the department associated with it. The sample position description in the exhibit indicates how a producer fits into the commercial insurance department. The description also summarizes some of the most important knowledge, experience, skills, and traits needed to perform effectively in the position.

A position description should be available for every position in the organization. Managers should be involved in developing and updating position descriptions because they are best qualified to determine the job requirements for employees who report to them. Defining position descriptions is also important for the training and development functions. Position descriptions create a catalog of skills required throughout the organization that must be maintained by training and development. Additionally, those who create and review position descriptions must be aware of the legal implications of the Americans with Disabilities Act (ADA) of 1990. Position descriptions should include only essential functions and must not include references to qualifications that are discriminatory to disabled persons. See the exhibit "Sample Position Description."

Position Qualifications

Position qualifications specify the requirements necessary to perform the responsibilities of the position. The qualifications should be written for an ideal candidate. Because the ideal employee may not be hired for the position, any qualification that the new employee does not possess becomes part of that person's individual training and development program. Therefore, careful attention must be given to developing the position qualifications.

The position qualifications should be based on the specific responsibilities listed in the position description. Also, the necessary knowledge, experience, skills, and any helpful personal traits summarized in the position description should be expanded.

For most responsibilities, a particular type of knowledge is necessary, and it should be included in the position description. For example, employees must have knowledge of the agency's management information system in order to enter and/or access customer data relevant to their particular job function. An experience requirement is also included in all but entry-level positions.

Frequently, skills are necessary in addition to knowledge. For the sample commercial insurance producer position, the employee must have the interpersonal and sales skills necessary to deal effectively with prospects and customers. Also, certain personal traits are helpful in certain jobs. For example, a producer needs to have a high energy level and persistence, a support staff employee needs to be detail oriented, and a person working in claims needs to be empathetic.

Sample Position Description

Position: Commercial Lines Producer

Reports to: Commercial Lines Manager

Department: Commercial Lines Department

Overall Responsibilities

This position is accountable for the production of new commercial lines business and the upgrading and retention of assigned commercial lines accounts.

Specific Responsibilities

1. Develop and maintain prospect file for new commercial insurance accounts.

2. Develop, maintain, and document contacts with prospects to gain information on expirations, insurance requirements, and receptiveness to proposals.

3. Conduct sales meetings, including developing account descriptions and needs, gathering underwriting information, and making presentations.

4. Coordinate the underwriting, placement, and financing of all new and renewal business with appropriate agency personnel.

5. Maintain contact with insured so that appropriate coverages are in force at renewal.

6. Develop, maintain, and expand professional relationships with insurer personnel and insureds.

7. Maintain communication with other agency production units to forward and receive information about insureds that may affect new commercial, personal, or life employee benefits business or indicate a change in insurability.

Nature and Scope

The Commercial Lines Department is charged with developing, placing, servicing, and renewing all commercial insurance accounts for the XYZ Agency. The producer is responsible for supporting departmental marketing activities as well as conducting individual marketing efforts at the Commercial Lines Manager's direction.

To maintain systematic growth by the Commercial Lines Department, the producer is responsible for maintaining accurate and up-to-date files and for documenting prospecting activities, account status, and sales and renewal activities.

The producer should possess strong written and oral communications skills, be well organized, exhibit a willingness to pursue professional studies, maintain a familiarity with industry trends and new insurance products, and have at least three years of commercial lines production experience.

[DA08093]

Evaluating Staffing Needs

An organization is adequately staffed when it has a sufficient number of employees with the appropriate skills to achieve organizational goals and objectives. Once job qualifications have been specified for all of the organization's positions, the organization must determine whether staffing is adequate. Adequate staffing is important to an organization because its ability to meet short-term and long-term goals and objectives is largely based on having the right people in place at the right time to implement plans. Staffing is also important for these reasons:

- Preparing for growth—Organizations that are adequately staffed are positioned for growth without the drawbacks that a staffing shortfall brings.
- Adapting to change—Organizations that are adequately staffed are flexible and are more adaptable to environmental changes than organizations that are not.
- Sustaining employee morale—An adequately staffed organization may prevent the poor employee morale that can accompany overwork and understaffing.

Organizations conduct several activities to maintain adequate staffing. These activities include these:

- Completing staffing projections
- Prospecting for employees
- Evaluating candidates
- Many organizations conduct these activities on a continuing basis, not just when a need arises.

Completing Staffing Projections

To ensure adequate staffing, an organization must determine its staffing needs by completing staffing projections for both current needs and for growth. An organization should determine the skills of current personnel and project how much growth the present organizational structure can accommodate, in part based on the number of current staff. Because existing staff may not be sufficient to attain a growth goal established during the planning process, a plan must be devised for hiring the necessary people and revising the organizational structure to support planned growth.

An organization depends on the abilities of its staff to meet goals and objectives. However, as growth is projected and related needs are assessed, the abilities required of an organization's current staff may change. The organization must evaluate whether its current staff can meet organizational goals and objectives and project staffing needs accordingly. Existing staff may be trained in new skills or cross-trained, or new employees with the required skills and experience may be hired.

Prospecting for Employees

Prospecting for employees on an ongoing basis can help ensure that adequate staffing is available when the need arises. Organizations often wait until a new employee is needed before beginning the hiring process. However, prospecting for employees in anticipation of future needs provides the organization with several benefits, including these:

- It increases the odds of selecting the right person by developing a pool of potential candidates.

- It saves administrative time, effort, and expense when a position becomes available.

- It helps the organization achieve a competitive edge in the face of a shrinking labor supply.

Prospective employees can be located from many sources, such as from within the agency, from other organizations, and from among recent high school and college graduates.

For example, an employee working within the agency in one position may be well suited to handle another position or may be eligible for a promotion. However, the same selection criteria used to evaluate external candidates should be applied to prospective internal employees.

Another source of prospective employees is other insurance organizations, including insurers, agencies, and professional and trade associations. Additionally, prospective employees could be available in organizations that are unrelated to insurance. People who prove to be good employees and demonstrate certain skill sets in one business are often effective in another.

Prospective employees may also be found among recent high school or college graduates. These prospects require more training than other prospective employees because they rarely have extensive knowledge or experience in dealing with business customers.

Depending on the resources available to assist with training, management must decide which of these sources to explore. If no time is available for training or if the manager has other priorities, recruiting experienced people—whether from inside or outside the organization—becomes the only option. The methods for prospecting are essentially the same for experienced and inexperienced employees.

Employers can identify prospects for employment by using various methods, including referrals; academic placement offices; employment agencies; and newspaper, magazine, or Internet advertisements.

Getting referrals from existing staff and other business sources is the best way to identify potential candidates. Two advantages of referrals are that finding people to interview is inexpensive and that some pre-screening has most likely already been done by the individual making the referral. Additionally, using the power of social networking to recruit new employees is a very inexpensive way to quickly get your message out to a targeted group of possible candidates.

High schools and colleges generally have placement offices that serve as clearing houses for students and employers. Sometimes these offices administer tests and provide other screening assistance for employers.

Employment agencies are also a good source of prospective employees. An obvious advantage of using reputable employment agencies is their effectiveness in screening prospective employees. However, employment agencies may charge a fee, which increases the total recruitment expense.

Newspaper, magazine, and Internet advertisements provide another source of prospective employees. The media must be selected carefully, and the wording of the ad must be chosen well. A carefully developed ad should reduce the number of time-consuming responses from unqualified prospects. The exhibit presents a sample ad designed to identify prospects for an agency's producer position, emphasizing the knowledge, skills, experience, and traits desired of such candidates.

Management Tip—One way to avoid spending time with unqualified prospective employees is to run a "blind ad"—one that asks prospects to send a resume to a post office box or a generic e-mail address and does not list the employer's name. Only prospects with the required knowledge, skills, experience, and traits need to be contacted, and this approach prevents unqualified prospects from contacting the organization.

Evaluating Candidates

Another activity in ensuring adequate staffing is evaluating candidates. The candidate evaluation process consists of these seven tasks:

1. Contacting candidates
2. Reviewing the job application
3. Interviewing candidates
4. Testing candidates
5. Checking references
6. Verifying candidates' experience and education
7. Offering employment

Only after this evaluation process is completed should a job offer be made. Skipping some of the tasks could save time, but more time and money could be spent (and wasted) if a poor hire is made.

The first task in the candidate evaluation process involves screening unqualified candidates from the pool of candidate responses received and contacting qualified candidates, either by telephone or in person. Those who are qualified should be asked to complete an application for employment. Those who are not qualified should be informed in writing. Prolonging the screening process is neither fair to the candidate nor a productive use of the manager's time.

The second task in the candidate evaluation process is reviewing the job application. Although some screening occurs during initial contact, the candidate's job application is the primary device for evaluating the candidate and frequently forms the basis for the manager's questions during the in-depth interview. Many organizations have their own job application form and may even have different forms for different job classifications. A good job application form that complies with federal regulations can help overcome the problems associated with discrimination in hiring. A question on an application is acceptable if it is job-related and if the information requested is necessary to determine whether the applicant could successfully perform the job.

The third task in the candidate evaluation process, interviewing candidates, is significantly affected by civil rights legislation, which governs the questions employers can ask job candidates. Such legislation puts the burden on the employer to ensure that the application and the interview/selection are not discriminatory on the basis of race, creed, sex, nationality, color, age, disability, or marital status. Questions in these areas that are not related to the job must not be part of the job application or the interview.

When hiring, employers must also consider the Americans with Disabilities Act (ADA) of 1990. This federal law prohibits discrimination in all employment practices against qualified individuals with disabilities in organizations with fifteen or more employees. The ADA requires employers to base employment decisions on the ability of the individual to perform the essential job functions, with or without reasonable accommodations. Reasonable accommodations include any modifications to the work facility, the application process, the job, or the manner in which the job is performed that do not place undue hardship on the employer.

Given the guidelines stipulated by the ADA, these are examples of questions that may not be asked before an offer of employment has been made to a candidate:

*   Do you have any disabilities that would affect your job performance?
*   How many days did you miss from work last year because of illness?
*   Have you ever submitted a workers' compensation claim?
*   Have you had any major illnesses in the last five years?

During the interview, however, employers are allowed to ask candidates to show how they would accomplish specific job tasks. For example, it would be permissible to ask an applicant with only one arm who has applied for a job as a data entry clerk to demonstrate how he or she would operate the computer with or without a reasonable accommodation. A basic assumption of the ADA is the degree to which nondisabled employers underestimate the ability of a disabled person to perform certain tasks. Rather than proving the disabled person is unfit for the job, a demonstration often proves the disabled person's ability to do the job.

Personal interview formats can vary from formal (structured) to informal (nonstructured) depending on management's preferences and the interviewer's skill.

Formal interviews are designed to overcome the problems many managers have in asking the right questions and correctly interpreting the answers. In one type of formal interview, carefully designed questions are used, and the interviewer records all the answers for later evaluation. For example, all candidates may be presented with an identical problem scenario and be asked to resolve it, such as, "You're already 30 percent under your commission goal for the year, and you've just heard that the agency lost its contract with its lead commercial insurer. What would you do?" Some critics believe that this type of formal interview is inflexible and that standard questions do not elicit enough information. Also, recording answers can create anxiety for the candidate.

In contrast to formal interviews, more informal, nonstructured interviews encourage applicants to talk freely, guided by questions from the interviewer. For instance, the question, "Tell me about a time when you had a successful sales experience," invites the applicant to talk freely about past business experiences. A major problem with the nonstructured interview is that it requires much more interpretive skill on the part of the interviewer to determine which information presented is relevant to the position.

Many organizations use a format that falls between formal and informal interviews, using predetermined guidelines and questions that allow the interviewer a degree of flexibility. When conducting an interview, the interviewer should try to picture the candidate in the position and be straightforward about the position and its responsibilities. An interviewer may become overly optimistic about a good candidate and may oversell the position instead of focusing on determining whether the candidate is best suited for the position.

When the interviewer has a clear set of position qualifications drawn from the position description and knows specifically what knowledge, experience, skills, and personality traits are required or desired, closed-ended questions will elicit specific answers, often a simple "yes" or "no." An example of a closed-ended question is, "Have you studied any insurance courses since your college graduation?"

Employers may conduct interviews in social situations, such as at a restaurant, to observe applicants in a relaxed setting. Salespeople are frequently expected to entertain customers, so interviewers may find it informative to include a social situation in the interviewing process to assess the applicant's level of comfort and skills in that environment.

The fourth task in the candidate evaluation process is testing the candidates. Several types of tests can be used, including:

- Personality or interest tests to reflect positive or negative aspects of the candidate's personality as they relate to the specific job and other employees in the organization

- Aptitude tests designed to measure the candidate's inherent ability for selling, detail work, or other essential job functions

- Knowledge tests to determine how much an applicant knows about the technical aspects of the job

- Intelligence tests intended to measure a candidate's innate intelligence

In addition, psychological tests are often used in the selection process for sales-related and management roles. If intelligence testing is used in the selection process, employers must ensure that such testing is properly administered and does not foster discriminatory practices. The Office of Federal Contract Compliance stipulates that tests should be professionally developed and validated if they are to be used in the selection process. As with the application and the interview, intelligence-test questions must be relevant to the position. The organization should keep records to show that the test is used to measure the candidate's ability to handle the position responsibilities.

The purpose of testing is to identify certain traits and qualifications that cannot be adequately measured by other selection tools. Although tests should not be a substitute for judgment, they can lend a measure of objectivity to the evaluation process. They are also used to provide a basis for interviewing, because any questionable characteristics highlighted in the test results may be explored further. Another reason for using employment tests is that they can help offset the high costs of hiring and training by increasing the chances of selecting people who will be effective and satisfied in the jobs they are hired to perform. Also, interpreting test results can identify an employee's personal development needs and provide the manager with additional insights to assist with that individual's professional development.

The fifth task in the candidate evaluation process is checking references. The employer may check both personal and business references. A visit, a telephone call, or a letter can be used, although many people providing references hesitate to put their comments in writing. Former customers, teachers, and business associates can be objective and reliable sources. Relatives and friends are generally not objective references.

Information obtained in references is seldom conclusive, but managers should not bypass this tool. A single significant fact uncovered may make the effort worthwhile. Some employers take the extra precaution of checking with a local credit bureau (with the applicant's written permission) to get additional information on the applicant's background and financial condition, particularly if the prospective employee is going to be involved with handling the organization's funds.

The sixth task in the candidate evaluation process is verifying candidates' experience and education. Employers should check candidates' work experience and educational achievements. Time taken to confirm the accuracy of such details is well spent. The employer must have reliable experience and education information to assist in predicting the candidates' ability to perform the job responsibilities.

The final task in the candidate evaluation process is offering employment. Once the hiring decision is made and feedback from the selected individual indicates that the candidate is seriously interested in employment, a formal employment offer is made. The offer may take the form of a detailed employment contract, or it may simply be a letter outlining the offer. Employers should be aware that offering employment to candidates is not always the last action required of managers. For example, a candidate may propose a counteroffer in the form of a higher starting salary or an increased benefits package or may negotiate a signing bonus. Managers should negotiate a response to such counteroffers until agreement is reached. In all cases, the employment terms should be described clearly in writing to protect all parties' interests.

ORGANIZATIONAL MANAGEMENT AND LEADING

An organization can have a sound plan, an effective organizational structure, and qualified employees, but unless managers are effective leaders, employees will not be as effective as they could be.

The skills required for leading in an insurance agency environment are similar to those required in a typical business environment, with perhaps more of a focus on certain skills required of the insurance producer entrepreneur. Skilled leadership promotes knowledgeable, dedicated employees working efficiently together to achieve the agency's goals and objectives.

These are the major aspects of leadership that are most important in an insurance agency environment:

- Motivating
- Delegating
- Managing conflict

Motivating

Motivation describes the psychological process that generates and sustains an individual's desire to achieve. Effective leaders, although not literally able to motivate employees by directing them to be motivated, can influence them and lead them toward achieving the organization's goals and objectives (and toward possible motivating rewards and activities the employees have identified as worthwhile).

Need is at the root of motivation; a desire to satisfy a need motivates action. If employees do not perceive that their needs can be satisfied, they have no incentive to act. For example, if a personal insurance CSR is told to start generating ten life insurance referrals per month but receives no commission from sales generated by the referrals, the CSR has no motivation to act. To motivate employees, the manager must be aware of these needs and must provide recognizable opportunities to satisfy them.

As used here, the word "need" includes both what a person must have and what a person wants. Individuals have physical needs for food and shelter, security needs for physical safety and economic well-being, social needs for status and a sense of belonging; and self-expression needs for personal accomplishment and the opportunity to grow. To a certain extent, how intensely people want something depends on what they already have and what they want. An individual's degree of need determines the strength of the desire, the level of motivation, and the resultant action.

One researcher into human behavior, Abraham Maslow, proposed a hierarchy of human needs, often represented as a pyramid. The bottom of the pyramid represents basic needs, and the top represents self-actualization needs. The lowest level of unmet needs on the pyramid is the prime human motivator. For example, hunger and thirst are needs at this lowest level. If the basic physiological needs of hunger and thirst are not satisfied, a person cannot be motivated to do anything other than seek food and water. Consequently, only one level of needs is primarily motivational at a time. In addition to the basic needs and self-actualization needs, Maslow's hierarchy includes safety needs, belongingness needs, and esteem needs.[1] For example, an employee with unmet esteem needs may be motivated through recognition, such as an employee of the month award.

Just as Maslow identified a hierarchy of needs, managers should recognize that their employees have various needs, which can be met in structured ways within the agency environment. To the extent that these needs are met, the agency and its employees meet their goals and objectives. Some of the more common needs in an agency setting are money, security, recognition, work importance and responsibility, status, advancement, goals, and incentives.

Money

Employees need to have enough money to satisfy physiological needs such as food, clothing, and shelter. Emotionally, employees need to earn enough money to have feelings of self-respect and security. Earning a comfortable living is in itself a motivator.

Wages should adequately reflect the difficulty and market value of a job. Money can be a destructive, negative factor if the salary level is perceived to be unfair relative to that provided by other organizations or relative to that provided to other employees in the same organization with similar responsibilities.

Security

People have a need to feel secure in the workplace. Employees who fear losing their jobs or who fear the financial collapse of the business spend time and energy worrying that could instead be directed toward working productively. Insecurity can develop in a small office, for example, after the loss of a large account or a sales slump that adversely affects agency income. Managers should be aware that ignoring employees' fears or attempting to conceal problems is likely to worsen the insecurity. Consistent, stable leadership and keeping employees informed of the agency's financial status are essential to satisfying the security need.

Recognition

Employees need to know that good work will be recognized by management. Recognition creates an atmosphere that reinforces and rewards outcomes that benefit the organization. Employees are more motivated to exhibit particular behaviors when a recognition system is in place. Positive reinforcement and recognition of individual accomplishments can be effective incentives, and they usually cost little in relation to their employee influence. When good performance is taken for granted, employees can become demotivated. Letting people know they are appreciated is not difficult; remembering to do so is harder. Recognition can take many forms, such as a public announcement, an award, or even a personal thank-you.

Work Importance and Responsibility

Employees need to feel that their work is important and that they have been given enough responsibility to make a contribution to the organization. In an agency setting, for example, if all emphasis is placed on the importance of the producer, then support personnel could feel as though their jobs are less important by comparison. Management must stress the importance of service in the production effort and must encourage the producers to do likewise. Support personnel who are recognized as crucial members of the production team can be motivated to reach much higher levels of performance and job satisfaction.

Status

Employees need to have an appropriate level of status in the organization, as evidenced by their fringe benefits, physical surroundings, and/or feedback. An assigned office, cubicle, or parking space; a certain title; or a territory of operations can provide such status. However, to some people, these aspects of status have little value. Instead, such persons focus on the respect and esteem of co-workers. To them, public praise for a job well done means more than a well-furnished corner office. Additionally, as organizations grow, managers can inadvertently threaten an individual's status by reassigning work in the interest of increased productivity. An employee who is responsible for certain tasks may feel a proprietary interest in handling them exclusively and may resist an offer of assistance even in times of heavy workload. This possibility does not mean that changes in assignments should not be made; however, the manager must be attuned to the possible reactions of the people involved in changes and should present the change in a way that reinforces rather than undermines the individual's status. For example, an individual could be made aware of how assigning some of that person's more basic tasks to another associate would give him or her valuable extra time for performing more complex duties.

Advancement

One of the most common reasons employees cite for quitting a job is that they had no opportunity to advance in the organization. Communicating and proving to employees that jobs will be filled from within when possible can help employee retention. If an agency adopts a career path, employees can be kept informed of how they can advance in the organization and of how they can increase their future income. Employees must be aware that any advancement opportunities will be available to them, and they must know what they can do to take advantage of them.

Goals

Employees need to have clearly defined goals and to know how to achieve them. Employee goals must be stated in absolute terms, and the employee's actions must be consistent with the goals. People have a natural desire to look forward to something. Therefore, managers should provide targets or expected results. Goals can be organizational, such as increasing new commission income, and supported by individual goals—for example, increasing the number of commercial customers. Goals can also be developmental, such as completing a professional designation. For the goals to be effective, the length of time between the goal-setting and the probable completion of the goals should be short enough for the individual to be able to visualize the result.

Incentives

Employees need incentives as motivators. Incentives affect both hiring and retention of quality employees. Managers can use incentives to influence employee performance, but only to the extent that the incentives meet the employees' needs. Incentives can be monetary or nonmonetary.

To motivate an employee, a monetary incentive must be viewed as both meeting an employee's need and reflecting the degree of work necessary to achieve it. Although the basic monetary incentive is salary, many organizations are broadening monetary incentives to include individual- or group-based performance incentives. For example, cash bonuses based on team or departmental achievement of certain established goals can be effective team motivators. Each employee's effort helps or hinders all other team members. Some managers find that quarterly bonuses provide better results than one year-end payment because frequent reinforcement is more effective as a motivator than long-term reinforcement.

Nonmonetary incentives can motivate all employees, but particularly those for whom money is not an effective motivator. These employees may reach a point at which they no longer want to work additional hours for additional rewards. For them, achieving balance between personal and professional life is more important than financial incentive. When an employee feels this way, the prospect of more money will not produce more work.

Nonmonetary incentives include:

- Benefits. Many agencies provide benefits packages of varying limits. Typical benefits include health insurance, life insurance, disability insurance, educational reimbursement, and a pension or retirement plan.

- Ownership. Some people are motivated by a desire to own their own business, either in whole or in part. For them, the agency ownership opportunity may be the most important incentive. Ownership opportunities can come in the form of shares earned as performance recognition, employee stock ownership plans (ESOPs), or simply the sale of shares in the agency to key employees as a means of agency perpetuation.

- Fringe benefits. Employees are motivated to a certain extent by fringe benefits or "perks" (everything but salary). Typical fringe benefits in insurance agencies include auto allowances (or a company car), expense accounts, and professional organization memberships.

- Time off. Vacations, holidays, and flexible work hours (flex time) are all effective nonmonetary employee incentives.

Although management must take the initiative in employee motivation, employees must also participate in creating a favorable work environment. Executives must recognize and respect the efforts of support personnel, and support personnel must recognize how every action they take can affect other employees and the organization's efforts to achieve its goals and objectives. Employees need to know they are instrumental in the group effort and that, as their workplace needs are being met, the potential for success of the organization is enhanced.

Management Tip—Popular incentives that some organizations now offer focus on child care and elder care. Many employees are single parents, are part of a two-income household, or are responsible for caring for aging family members. When a parent has to take time off from work to care for a child, it can cause a serious emotional as well as financial strain. The same can be true when employees are responsible for an aging parent or another family member. Providing flexible working hours to enable employees to see their children off to school or granting additional time off to supplement a home healthcare worker's hours can be perceived as a significant benefit. One business turned a room in its building into a nursery/clinic staffed by a medically trained childcare worker. Another offered vouchers for a local home nursing service so that someone could stay with a sick child at home while the parent came to work. Employers can consider asking their employees with children or aged or disabled relatives what they can do to help.

Delegating

Delegating is a second major aspect of leadership that is important in an agency environment. Delegating is the art of getting work done through other people by giving them responsibility and authority to do the work. Delegation is one of the most difficult activities for many managers to handle effectively, particularly managers who were promoted from a position within the department they now manage. Such managers are accustomed to doing the work themselves.

Management Tip—A critical error managers often make is doing only half of what is required for effective delegation: freely distributing responsibility for the work but retaining the authority to do the work. Employees cannot be given the manager's work without the authority to accomplish that work. Effective delegation means transferring the work and the authority as well.

The key to effective delegation is for managers to lead by communicating clearly and concisely when delegating a task. The manager must state expected results and clearly define the scope of the authority and responsibility. Because the manager does not delegate all authority or abdicate the ultimate responsibility, information must flow between the manager and the employee to ensure that the employee has enough information to make decisions and to use the delegated authority effectively.

In addition, the chain of command must be clearly understood. Communication is essential. Employees must know who is delegating what work to them and to whom to refer matters that exceed their authority. For example, an insurance agency owner leaving town on an extended business trip may lead by delegating management of the entire agency's operations to the agency operations manager until the owner returns. Failure to communicate this information to the operations manager's counterpart, the sales manager, could create conflict between those two employees.

Managing Conflict

Managing conflict is a third major aspect of leadership in an agency environment. Sometimes a manager must act as a mediator in settling differences between employees. Conflicts can arise because of different personalities, different opinions on how to perform a particular task, and other factors. A manager should be objective when dealing with differences that arise between employees; a manager who is not impartial will lose respect and, consequently, become less effective as a manager. Some disagreements are temporary and can be resolved quickly and easily. However, sometimes individuals find it impossible to coexist in the same organization. Unpleasant but necessary action, such as probation or even termination, may have to be taken for the benefit of the agency staff.

Integrative bargaining

A negotiation strategy by which the parties in a conflict work together to understand their relationship, their interests, their respective perceptions, and their attitudes in order to achieve a mutually satisfactory resolution.

Distributive negotiation

Adversarial negotiation in which the parties compete for resources while conceding little to the negotiation process.

Managers can use negotiation to resolve many conflicts. Negotiation involves discussing the issue in conflict and considering alternatives with the aim of reaching a mutual agreement.

Integrative bargaining is a form of cooperative negotiation in which the parties in conflict work together to achieve a mutually satisfactory resolution. In contrast, an example of **distributive negotiation** is as an employee negotiating for a raise from an employer who has had a financially difficult year.

Five strategies are available to managers to use as needed in their organizations to manage conflict, facilitate integrative bargaining, and avoid the negativity of distributive negotiation. These five strategies are:[2]

1. Emphasize superordinate goals
2. Focus on the problem, not the people
3. Focus on interests, not demands
4. Create new options for joint gain
5. Focus on what is fair

Emphasize Superordinate Goals

Superordinate goals are goals that both managers and employees can agree to in order to achieve a greater organizational purpose, regardless of the sources of conflict. For example, an agency can emphasize quality customer service, increasing sales, or improving customer retention at the same time as dealing with an integrative bargaining issue such as whether to implement flex time.

Keeping superordinate goals paramount helps both negotiating parties remember that they are part of a larger organization with a shared mission that must be fulfilled, despite any differences at a lower level.

Focus on the Problem, Not the People

When a manager is confronted with differences regarding employees, the conflict should not be personalized. The focus should be on the problem or the source of the conflict, not on personal flaws or deficiencies. For example, if a manager accuses a nonperforming CSR of being lazy, rather than considering that problems may exist with the agency's workflow, then the negotiation immediately moves toward an adversarial, distributive negotiation instead of an integrative solution.

Focus on Interests, Not Demands

Immediate demands of both parties may be difficult to meet in a conflict situation. However, a manager can seek to understand the parties' underlying interests and meet their underlying needs, establishing the basis of integrative negotiation.

For example, assume a manager institutes a program requiring that the agency's in-house CSRs generate a certain percentage of new-business sales per month through cross-selling and account development. The new program creates conflict because the manager demands new-business sales and the CSRs demand that they be allowed to continue in a service-only role. Through negotiation, the manager discovers that the CSRs' underlying interest is a concern that focusing on sales will limit the time available to them to serve customers. The manager proposes a solution that addresses the CSRs' underlying interest: contracting the servicing of a portion of their personal and small commercial accounts to an insurer customer call center. The CSRs can then focus on generating new-business sales while having their underlying interests met. Consequently, the manager's interest in generating new-business sales is also achieved.

Create New Options for Joint Gain

When two parties involved in a conflict agree on interests rather than demands, they create a "win-win" environment that often generates additional, more creative solutions to the conflict than those first envisioned. Other optional resources and alternatives may be considered, thereby leading the organization and its personnel to greater profitability, that is, joint gain.

For instance, using the previous new-business example, the manager may decide to pay the CSRs a bonus based on every policy sold per month over a particular minimum number. The bonus incentive motivates CSRs to improve their cross-selling and account development, and the manager pays the bonus from the commissions received from the additional policies sold—a "win-win" situation.

Focus on What Is Fair

It is understandable that managers and employees may disagree on certain points when discussing differences and that they may be inclined to emphasize the alternatives that support their respective views. However, focusing on fairness assists both parties in arriving at mutually agreeable solutions.

Producers have responsibilities both to their customers and to insurers to conduct business in a fair manner. For example, an agency should not move its book of business from one insurer to another simply because the new insurer offers a higher-percentage commission. Policy forms should be compared, and the insurers' claim services and policyholder services should be assessed, as well as many other factors. Only after thorough consideration should the agency consider moving its book of business, and even then the agency may decide to move the business only on a customer-by-customer basis, keeping each customer's best interests foremost in mind. Such an approach conveys a sense of fairness to employees—in this case, producers—and minimizes conflict.

Although managing conflict is important, controlling an organization is equally important to enable the organization to reach its goals and objectives.

ORGANIZATIONAL MANAGEMENT AND CONTROLLING

Controlling is the function by which managers establish accurate measuring and monitoring systems to evaluate how well the organization has achieved its goals and objectives. It includes the employee performance evaluation process.

Some managers believe the controlling function is limited to checking on a person's production or an activity, but it involves considerably more. Control is used to influence employee behavior and is the vital follow-up to planning, organizing, and leading because it monitors the results of those functions. Control is essential to good management.

Managers who evaluate employees against performance standards often do so in the context of a formal employee performance evaluation, a tool with which managers objectively assess employee performance. Managers use the control process to monitor the organization and to keep staff focused on organizational goals and objectives.

Control Process

Organizations use control not only to respond to events after they have occurred, but also to keep staff motivated and focused on organizational goals. The control process consists of four steps:

1. Establishing performance standards against which performance is to be evaluated
2. Measuring results
3. Comparing results against chosen performance standards
4. Evaluating the results and implementing corrective action if the performance standards are not being met

Establishing Performance Standards

The first step in the control process is establishing performance standards (benchmarks) against which performance is to be evaluated. Standards usually involve employee performance results (individually and as a group), financial results, and sales results. The performance standards that organizations establish could measure different variables, such as efficiency, innovation, quality, and customer responsiveness. For example, an agency could establish the performance standard of processing commercial insurance renewals and offering renewal ninety days before the account's renewal date. Another agency could establish a performance standard that sets specific producer new-business sales goals.

Reporting systems gather and present information in a format useful for measuring results. These systems should be simple and should allow for easy comparison of results. Reports that are excessively time-consuming to prepare may not be valuable in the long run because of their adverse effect on employee or manager productivity. Reports should always be in writing.

Control reports are meant to present a comparison of performance against an established standard and to reveal improvement or decline. They should contain only key comparisons, measuring an employee's efficiency, quality of work, and responsiveness to customers in operational areas. Reports should be developed to measure an agency's selected key operational areas, such as new business commission per producer, for which measurable standards can be developed.

Measuring Results

The second step in the control process is measuring the results. Managers can evaluate organizational and individual employee results in two areas: (1) outputs—for example, a manager could measure the number of new business policies sold and (2) activities—for example, the number of prospects visited.

Measuring results provides an objective comparison of the organization's and the employee's performance against standards. For example, if the agency does not meet its sales goals, a sales manager might examine the producers' activity reports and consider these questions:

- How much time are the producers spending in the office as opposed to going out on prospect visits?
- How many sales calls were made?
- What are the producers' hit ratios?
- What external events (such as regulation changes or a decrease in available insurers) prevented the agency and individual employees from achieving standards?

Comparing Results With Chosen Performance Standards

The third step in the control process is comparing the results against chosen performance standards. Are employees, and the organization, succeeding? Are performance standards being met, or is performance lower or higher than expected?

Managers may take the opportunity to evaluate and revise the performance standards at this time. Specifically, they might ask these questions about the performance standards:

- Were the standards set so high that they were unattainable?
- Were the standards set so low that they were accomplished too easily?
- Did external changes (such as a major competitor's move into the geographic area) affect the employees' and the organization's ability to achieve performance standards?

Depending on the answers to these and similar questions, the performance standards may require revision. The manager typically revises performance standards, evaluates results, and implements corrective action, if necessary.

Evaluating Results and Implementing Corrective Action

The fourth step in the control process is evaluating results and implementing corrective action if the performance standard is not being met. First, the manager must evaluate why the performance standard was not met. The reason for not meeting the standard dictates what corrective action should be taken. Failing to meet a sales standard, for instance, may have resulted from internal issues such as insufficient training or an insufficient number of calls on qualified prospects.

To correct these problems, the manager may require additional training or may establish specific goals and criteria for weekly prospect calls. Failure to recognize internal issues during this evaluation phase may result in applying the wrong solutions to correct the problems, which could be a costly error for any organization.

In contrast, if performance standards are being met or exceeded, an organization may continue with its current performance standards, with little if any corrective action required.

Employee Performance Evaluation

Anyone who manages or supervises employees is responsible for providing them with an evaluation of their performance. Whether it shows success or the need for improvement, the evaluation must be objective and accurate.

Performance evaluation starts with setting goals for the employee, generally on an annual basis with interim evaluations. To be effective, these goals should be developed following the "SMART" approach. Each goal should be specific, measurable, achievable, relevant, and time bound. The goal-setting process should be collaborative, with the manager and employee working together to establish goals. Goals for individual employees should be based on the organization's overall goals and objectives and support its established strategy.

By establishing goals for the employee, the manager is setting expectations for job performance and desired behaviors. In addition to establishing goals, the performance plans should include opportunities for development, such as training programs or participation in special projects, work teams, or task forces. Discussions between the manager and employee can identify appropriate development areas based on organizational and department needs as well as the employee's current skills and his or her specific strengths and interests.

Factors considered in performance evaluation include not only whether goals—such as number of accounts serviced or established sales goals—have been met, but also whether skill levels in areas such as written and oral communication are strong. Such skills are usually ranked on a scale using a defined range and terms such as excellent to poor, with intervals of very good, good, and fair. Other methods may include a numerical scale such as one to five, with five being the highest available rating and one the lowest.

Formal performance appraisals should occur at least annually and provide feedback of the performance evaluation to the employee. This feedback communicates to the employee where they are meeting or exceeding established goals and areas where improvement may be required. Feedback may be based solely on the manager's appraisal or may include input from co-workers or subordinates within the same department. Evaluations may also be solicited from insurers or customers outside of the organization or from co-workers in other departments within the organization who frequently interact with the employee.

Performance evaluation should not be limited to formal annual or semi-annual appraisals. The manager should provide frequent feedback to the employee to reinforce positive behavior or to address problems as they arise.

SUMMARY

The four functions of management are: planning, leading, organizing, and controlling. Planning involves identifying and selecting organizational goals and objectives and the means to best achieve them. An organization ensures optimal performance through the planning process. Effective plans have certain characteristics.

Large organizations have three major types of plans—corporate, business, and functional—and all should be consistent with the organization's goals and objectives. Organizations typically use a seven-step planning process to create their plans: develop a mission statement, develop goals, develop strategies, develop objectives, develop budgets, establish policies and procedures, and monitor the plan.

The management function of organizing includes deciding on organizational structure. Once the structure of the organization has been determined, managers develop position descriptions and then evaluate staffing needs for the organization.

Once the organizational structure has been established, managers develop position descriptions for required staffing needs. Position descriptions are written summaries of particular jobs in an organization. They describe the position of a job in the organization, overall responsibilities, the position's specific responsibilities, and the nature and scope of the job within its associated department.

Effective leadership includes three major aspects: motivating, delegating, and managing conflict.

Controlling is the management function of measuring and monitoring activities to evaluate how well the organization has achieved its goals. Managers must ensure that employee performance evaluations are objective and accurate.

ASSIGNMENT NOTES

1. Gareth R. Jones and Jennifer M. George, Contemporary Management (New York: McGraw-Hill Higher Education, 2009), p. 472.

2. Jones and George, p. 614.

Direct Your Learning ▶▶

Agency Sales Management

Educational Objectives

After learning the content of this assignment, you should be able to:

▷ Describe the purposes of agency sales management.

▷ Describe top-down and bottom-up agency sales management systems.

▷ Describe the steps in the sales management process.

▷ Describe the three steps involved in establishing a sales management organizational structure.

▷ Explain why an agency plans for the following in order to meet its strategic goals:

  • Staffing the agency

  • Hiring new producers

  • Developing new and existing producers

▷ Explain how an agency uses the following aspects of sales management operations in order to meet its strategic goals:

  • Producer compensation systems

  • Producer performance and accountability

▷ Given a scenario regarding an agency sales manager meeting with the agency's producers, determine how both planning and operational elements discussed in the meeting contribute towards the agency's overall strategic goals.

▶▶

Agency Sales Management

AGENCIES AND SALES MANAGEMENT

Insurance agencies are primarily sales organizations. Therefore, an agency's sales management must be a key component of the overall management of the agency.

Sales management is the planning, leading, organizing, and controlling of sales efforts to achieve the agency's strategic goals. Sales managers and agency owners direct and guide producers through a variety of functions. The agency's managers must also determine, based on the agency's strategic plan and customer needs, the type of sales system and organizational structure that best meets those needs.

Agencies focused on fully using their resources typically dedicate at least one individual to a sales management position, such as marketing director or manager, sales director or manager, or vice president of sales and marketing. Although the person who directs an agency's sales process may have a variety of titles, in this discussion that person will be referred to as the agency sales manager. Agency sales managers coordinate selling with other elements of total marketing programs. Sales managers are responsible for the general sales force administration, and they are also involved in setting year-to-year sales and marketing goals, planning programs to achieve those goals, and evaluating results.

Dedicating at least one employee to the agency sales manager position helps fulfill the two purposes of agency sales management:

- To maximize the agency's production efforts
- To promote effectiveness and efficiency when selling insurance products and providing service to insureds

Maximize Production Efforts

The primary purpose of agency sales management is to maximize production efforts. However, when an agency attempts to accomplish the purpose by appointing its best producer to be the agency sales manager while continuing to act as a producer, this can create dual-role inefficiencies. Producers may neither want nor enjoy the dual role of producer and manager but may have to assume it because of the agency's size and resources. The result is often a decrease in the producer/agency sales manager's production.

For example, consider a small agency in which the agency producer principal acts as the informal sales manager. The agency typically needs little overall management because of its size, and the principal can continue to sell as well as manage the agency. With a small, motivated staff, this simple management system works well for a time. However, if an ambitious new agency producer or a growing community causes the agency's sales to increase, the principal eventually must spend more time managing the agency's growing staff and less time selling. The agency may add two more producers to deal with the principal's sales workload. The principal may then decide that the agency needs a sales manager. Rather than hiring an individual with training and experience in a sales management position, the principal would often opt for what seems to be the obvious solution: assign the position to the agency's top producer. This producer is already familiar with the agency, and the principal believes that promoting the producer to management rewards the producer for outstanding achievement.

The likely outcome in this example is a decrease in sales after the producer is promoted because of the loss of an experienced producer and dissatisfaction among the other producers because of an inexperienced manager. Facing this deteriorating situation, the principal must make a decision: whether to keep the agency sales manager in this position and risk further problems or to return the manager exclusively to sales and resume the management function. Neither decision represents a good solution to the problems caused by the producer's promotion.

The agency principal could have avoided this situation by hiring a full-time agency sales manager who has management training and who is given no production responsibilities. Many principals do not make this choice for various reasons, including an unwillingness to relinquish management control and a concern that the additional personnel cost cannot be justified in addition to a lack of industry or technical experience among managerial candidates. To develop an understanding of the cost/benefit relationship of assigning the agency sales manager position to a successful producer, agency principals and producers can use an analysis such as this:

> Assume that a principal or producer can generate an average of $200 per hour in sales commissions. If that principal or producer spends 15 hours per week on sales management activities, the agency is deprived of $3,000 per week ($200 per hour × 15 hours per week) in additional revenue, which could be used to pay an agency sales manager's salary. If the agency's current expense level (before commission to producers) is 50 percent, then $1,500 per week would be available to pay a new agency sales manager without the agency's surrendering any current profits. If an agency sales manager can run the agency for a total compensation of less than $1,500 per week, then the agency would profit more by hiring the agency sales manager.

Another option for an agency that does not have the resources or prefers not to hire an agency sales manager with no production responsibility is to develop IT solutions to assist with sales management.

Promote Effectiveness and Efficiency

Another purpose of agency sales management is to promote effectiveness and efficiency. Agency sales management must be effective because success in selling insurance products and providing service is crucial to the agency's ongoing success. It must be efficient because the cost of sales force management is typically the largest single insurance agency operating expense. Efficient sales management helps reduce or eliminate wasted time and expense resulting from duplication of effort, inadequate staffing or training, and misdirected resources.

There are a number of IT systems available to provide more effective and efficient sales management for an agency. These are typical features of such systems:

- Client information and customer service applications
- Interface with insurer systems
- Commission calculation and tracking
- Agency sales goals and performance
- Individual producer sales goals and performance

Increasingly, agents and insurers do business over the Internet, and agency IT systems can increase the effectiveness of cyber-relationships with insurers. These systems can also provide alerts for policy delivery, customer service follow-up after a sale, renewals, and other key customer activities. Sales and commission reports can be generated. Producers' performance can be tracked against goals.

SALES MANAGEMENT SYSTEMS

Managers considering their options for sales management systems have two categories of systems to choose from: top-down and bottom-up.

Whether an agency's managers choose a top-down or bottom-up system can determine the type of information technology (IT) system the agency selects. Conversely, the agency's IT system can influence the choice of top-down or bottom-up sales management. Either type of management system can result in successful sales if there is IT system support and consensus on goals between producers and management. See the exhibit "Agency Management Focus."

Agency Management Focus

An agency's focus determines both the types of insurance it will produce as well as the management style and culture of an agency. This focus can also determine how successful the agency will be.

Costello & Sons Insurance (CSI) in San Francisco began a new, innovative approach and more than doubled revenues over a six-year period. Bryan Costello, the agency's owner, said, "What has made all of this possible is the people that we have. They are involved in all the decisions we make and know exactly how we are doing."

Dennis H. Pillsbury, "Building a World-Class Agency," Rough Notes, May 2011, www.roughnotes.com/rnmagazine/05cdindex11.htm (accessed September 21, 2011). [DA08067]

Top-Down Systems

Top-down system

A system in which management sets the long-range and annual sales goals for the agency and determines how they will be achieved.

Some agencies use a **top-down system** for sales management. Producers are given specific goals (for example, $250,000 in new business commissions over the next year, a 90 percent retention rate on renewals, and twenty-five new expiration dates per week) to help the agency reach its overall goals. In large organizations, the goals work their way down through several levels. See the exhibit "Top-Down Sales Management System—XYZ Agency, 200X."

Management then periodically monitors producers and branch offices to ensure they are on target for achieving their goals. Small agencies may have only one or two producers to meet the agency's goals, and those goals are relatively simple to administer and control. For example, if an agency with two producers has the goal, "We will increase our new business commissions by 20 percent this year," then each of the two producers will readily understand the goal.

An agency with a top-down sales management focus should use IT systems that have a similar framework to support the agency's sales management. The types of reports available through the system would include tracking of agency and producer sales results against goals. Small agencies with basic computer systems may find that these types of technological systems are most supportive of traditional top-down sales management.

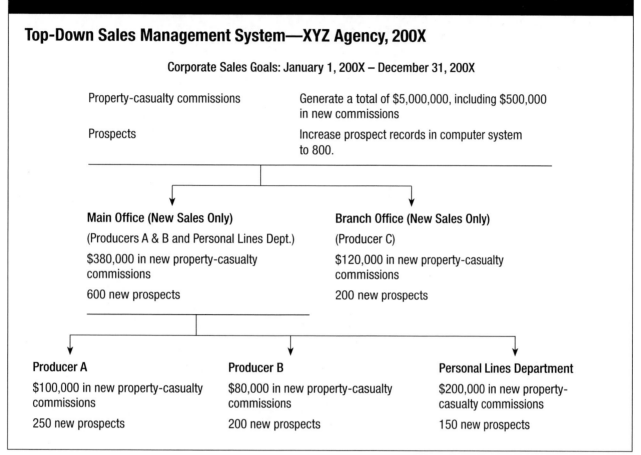

Top-Down Sales Management System—XYZ Agency, 200X

Corporate Sales Goals: January 1, 200X – December 31, 200X

Property-casualty commissions	Generate a total of $5,000,000, including $500,000 in new commissions
Prospects	Increase prospect records in computer system to 800.

Main Office (New Sales Only)

(Producers A & B and Personal Lines Dept.)

$380,000 in new property-casualty commissions

600 new prospects

Branch Office (New Sales Only)

(Producer C)

$120,000 in new property-casualty commissions

200 new prospects

Producer A

$100,000 in new property-casualty commissions

250 new prospects

Producer B

$80,000 in new property-casualty commissions

200 new prospects

Personal Lines Department

$200,000 in new property-casualty commissions

150 new prospects

[DA08069]

Bottom-Up Systems

Some agencies manage sales with a **bottom-up system**, which involves producers and branch managers in larger agencies in setting both individual and agency sales goals. These agencies may organize meetings to discuss the types and amount of business they plan to produce during the coming year. The degree to which producers are involved in goal setting varies by agency. In larger agencies, the information flows from small agency units through large agency units, and from producers to production departments through multiple offices.

The IT systems used by agencies with a bottom-up focus must be able to provide the data and reports to support this type of sales management. Various systems are available for insurance agencies that provide real-time information on the agency's sales performance as well as market information.

Bottom-up system

A system that uses aggregate sales information from agency units, producers, and branch offices to create overall agency goals.

AGENCY SALES MANAGEMENT PLANNING— DEVELOPING A PROCESS

Because an agency's sales are the key to the agency's success, it is important for an agency's managers to develop a plan for setting and reaching sales goals.

A seven-step process can be used by an agency's managers to develop and implement a sales plan:

1. Develop a mission statement
2. Develop goals
3. Develop strategies
4. Develop objectives
5. Develop budgets
6. Establish policies and procedures
7. Evaluate results

Develop a Mission Statement

An agency's mission statement is a broad statement of the agency's purpose and overarching goals. An example of an agency mission statement is, "Our agency will provide superior service to our customers, our community, and our insurer partners." The sales mission statement in support of this overall mission might be, "Our producers will provide outstanding service, knowledge, and products to insure that our customers are protected."

The mission statement frames a vision for the agency and its producers. Some agencies require their sales managers to develop a personal mission statement with each producer that is consistent with the agency's mission but has an individual perspective. An example of such a statement might be, "I will search for ways to increase insurance protection for my current customers and to expand this protection into my community."

A mission implies a belief, and mission statements are important because they frame the beliefs and purpose of an organization's work. There is a difference between merely "selling a product" and "providing an important good or service." Producers who believe in the value of what they and their agency are doing are more likely to be successful.

Develop Goals

The second step in the sales management process is to develop specific goals. Sales goals are developed using "SMART" (specific, measurable, achievable, relevant, time-bound) criteria. An example of an agency's sales goal is to increase annual net new-business personal insurance commissions by 20 percent.

An agency sales manager may develop several sales goals as part of the sales management process. Agency goals change from year to year as goals are achieved and as the sales management process is evaluated.

Develop Strategies

The third step in the sales management process is to develop sales strategies. Strategies evolve from the broader agency goals. Typical insurance agency sales strategies involve premium volume, business mix, or specialization. Premium volume strategies are designed to increase the agency's volume to a planned level. Business mix strategies involve a plan to change the mix of agency business, for example, to decrease emphasis on sales in one area (such as commercial insurance) and increase sales in another area (such as health and disability insurance). Specialization strategies may include growth in narrowly defined areas, such as professional liability insurance, or growth in a predetermined market, such as the agency's current customers.

A practical example of a specialization strategy is an agency's decision to develop risk control and risk financing services and offer them to its customers and prospects. The agency believes this is a viable strategy because its market consists of businesses generating $2 million to $50 million in sales. Businesses of this size typically are not large enough to have their own risk management departments.

Develop Objectives

The fourth step in the sales management process is to develop objectives. Objectives are specific targets and milestones that enable the agency and producers to achieve the agency's mission and goals. Like goals, objectives are developed using the "SMART" criteria. For example, a producer objective directed toward meeting agency sales goals would be to produce five new commercial accounts per week and to obtain three referrals from each new-business account sold. See the exhibit "The Importance of Sales Planning."

The Importance of Sales Planning

The Independent Insurance Agents of America (IIAA) Best Practices Study found that a weakness among leading insurance agencies was poor sales planning. The study also found that effective agency management was one of the keys to success.

Phil Zinkewicz, IIAA's Best Practices Study gauges strengths and weaknesses of agencies and companies," Rough Notes, www.roughnotes.com/rnmagsearchndx.htm (accessed September 22, 2011). [DA08116]

Develop Budgets

The fifth step in the sales management process is to develop budgets. Although the most common aspect of budgeting is to allocate money in a way that best serves the agency's goals, the allocation of people and time is also an important aspect of budgeting. Just as the agency sales manager allocates available funds, the sales manager should allocate the producers' and CSRs' time.

Time required to perform sales and sales-related activities varies by agency and should be adjusted according to agency and producer needs. As sales increase, management should plan a budget for allocating additional support staff.

Establish Policies and Procedures

The sixth step in the sales management process is to establish policies and procedures. Agency sales managers sometimes establish the policies and procedures; for example, they may determine how producers should solicit new business. Other examples of common policies relating to sales management include these:

- Obtain a 25 percent down payment (minimum) to accompany all new business applications.
- Transfer servicing of all commercial accounts generating premiums under $5,000 annually to the Small Accounts Unit.
- Review renewal of personal insurance V.I.P. accounts with producers and CSRs; all other renewals are the sole responsibility of personal insurance CSRs.

Policies such as these define the general work rules and tell agency personnel what to do in certain situations. They help facilitate work flow and accelerate transaction processing by eliminating the need to make repeated decisions relating to certain activities. Policies and procedures are often drawn from insurer recommendations and best practices, errors and omissions (E&O) insurer requirements, and the agency's own history of proven best practices.

A growing agency may overlook the importance of written sales procedures. Pressures of daily work can often take precedence over creating procedures. The result of this focus can be duplication of effort and inefficient processing, which affect both sales and servicing. Consequently, producers spend less time generating new business and more time, for example, trying to solve late payment problems or working on small accounts that a CSR could handle.

Agencies with well-structured sales management systems provide written procedures for producers that facilitate training and help maintain quality control. See the exhibit "XYZ Agency, Inc., New Prospect Contact Procedures."

Evaluate Results

The seventh step in the agency sales management planning process is to evaluate the results and the effectiveness of the agency's sales plan. The sales manager can make any necessary corrections and work with producers

XYZ Agency, Inc., New Prospect Contact Procedures

Sample of Agency New Prospect Procedures

Position: Commercial Lines Producer

Function: Initial call on prospect

1. Make presentation that reviews the insurance programs available through the agency; risk control emphasis, billing plans, and the stability of the agency and/ or insurers.

2. If the response from prospect is yes:

a. Gather information on prospect: current coverage and policies, expiration dates, and general information needed for quoting the business.

b. Set time to return for presentation.

c. Submit information to commercial insurance accounts assistant for proposal preparation and insurer marketing.

d. Log into agency management system prospect database.

If the response from prospect is no:

a. Obtain expiration dates.

b. Thank prospect for time.

c. Make notes on loss exposures.

d. Update prospect system.

e. Re-solicit at follow-up date notification from system.

3. Proceed to a formal proposal.

[DA08117]

during the agency's business year to make plan adjustments. The agency sales manager monitors the plan by examining individual weekly and monthly production reports, conducting sales meetings, and determining how results compare to the plan's goals.

SALES MANAGEMENT ORGANIZATIONAL STRUCTURE

A well-organized sales organization is structured to help individual producers and the overall agency achieve their sales goals. Additionally, the sales organization helps producers and support personnel to interact effectively.

Sales organizations such as insurance agencies are not static; they must be able to adapt to changes. At various stages in its life cycle, the agency may have to alter its organizational structure to accommodate growth or market changes, yet remain true to its fundamental focus in sales. An agency needs to be flexible enough to handle change yet stable enough to withstand the inevitable stresses that accompany market changes.

Each agency should determine the type of sales structure that will best meet the agency's sales goals and other management objectives. Establishing an organizational structure involves three distinct steps:

- Define and assign responsibilities.
- Group responsibilities by position.
- Determine job interrelationships.

Types of Agency Sales Structures

An insurance agency can be set up according to any organizational structure, but certain structures have proved more effective for sales than others. These are typical organizational structures used by insurance agencies:

- Line of business, such as commercial or personal lines
- Functional teams, such as producers, customer service representatives, informational technology (IT), and accounting
- Insurer, in those agencies that place business with several key insurers
- Premium or revenue volume
- Account, such as an alphabetical or a geographical assignment of customers
- A hybrid, combining two or more of these

Define and Assign Responsibilities

When establishing a sales management organizational structure, management must define and assign responsibility to producers and support staff for the major activities associated with the sales function. For an agency producing property-casualty insurance, these activities can include sales management, property-casualty sales, new and renewal business placement with insurers, policy rating and quoting, other customer service support of the sales process, accounting services and support, IT support of the overall sales process (including marketing support and accountability tools), and administrative services. When examining an existing agency's organizational structure, management must disregard the current structure and list the responsibilities performed, regardless of existing positions or individuals handling those responsibilities.

Managers can begin defining sales responsibilities by examining a producer's job description. Insurance agencies are sales organizations, and all responsibilities performed in the organization ultimately support the producer and the sales function. Producers have eight key accountabilities that are necessary to sell to and retain customers:

- Prospecting—The sales process begins with prospecting. Producers should build and maintain a database of potential customers. In most property-casualty agencies, each producer is responsible for prospecting. However, to maximize producers' selling time, many agency managers have shifted prospecting duties to other agency employees or to outside services.

- Fact-finding—Insurance sales are based on matching insurance products and services with prospects' specific needs. Fact finding mainly involves loss exposure identification, which is the basis of the customer's needs. The fact-finding process may include physically inspecting the prospect's operations and premises, completing survey forms, drawing flowcharts of operations, reviewing the prospect's marketing materials and Web site, and researching financial statements to determine which assets need protection.

- Sending the submission to the underwriter—Once the prospect's needs have been identified, the producer is ultimately accountable for obtaining premium quotations for requested coverages by submitting the information to the underwriter. Most agencies have Internet access to insurers, and a customer service representative (CSR) or administrative assistant may submit information to underwriters. Producers, however, are ultimately responsible for obtaining timely quotations for their prospects.

- Preparing proposals—After producers have received premium quotes from underwriters, they may prepare and present proposals. These proposals can range from informal discussion of competing quotes to a formal meeting with a slide or video presentation. There are various types of software that agencies and producers can use with their information technology (IT) systems to produce presentations. Additionally, insurers may have marketing and presentation tools available.

- Presenting proposals—Clarity is important in the presentation of the proposal to the prospect—the prospect must be able to readily understand the information presented. Using insurance language such as "ACV," "products liability," or "coinsurance" may confuse some prospects. Using illustrations, examples, and understandable language is essential when presenting a complex technical insurance proposal.

- Closing—Closing, or asking for the sale, is vital because few people will purchase if they are not asked to make the purchase. Although some agencies use inside technical or support people to help with all or part of the proposal, closing is solely the producer's responsibility.

- Providing initial customer service—All aspects of customer service include meeting the needs of the customer from the customer's perspective. Initial customer service includes, but is not limited to, ensuring that applications are completed and signed, collecting payment, and issuing a binder along with a binder bill. Sometimes the producer handles only the first of these activities, and others in the agency deal with the rest. The initial service is essential in establishing a positive, long-term customer relationship.

- Providing long-term customer service—Once the policy has been issued, the producer must see that it is delivered to the insured, plan regular contacts with the insured, and arrange for audits, if required. Before policy renewal, new information on operations should be gathered and renewal questionnaires reviewed. Claims may require follow-up action. Responsibilities associated with long-term customer service, such as audits and claim handling, should be carefully assigned and supervised to meet (and, whenever possible, exceed) the customer's expectations. Meeting and exceeding customer expectations can help maintain and perhaps increase the customer's business with the agency.

How these accountabilities are assigned between producers and support staff varies among agencies. Also, an agency's technology can be used to assist with certain aspects of these functions, such as submitting information to underwriters.

Group Responsibilities by Position

After defining and assigning responsibilities, the agency must group them by position. Grouping responsibilities into positions maximizes the agency's use of the human and economic resources that support the sales management organization.

How responsibilities are assigned depends on the size of the agency. For example, a relatively small agency may have to combine some responsibilities into one multi-function position because any one of the responsibilities would not keep an individual occupied full-time. Consequently, one position may involve both sales and sales management. Large agencies can afford to employ persons to specialize within a major activity. Producers, for example, are frequently differentiated by type of business (such as professional liability specialists or benefits specialists) or by type of account (such as agricultural or manufacturing). Generally, the larger the agency, the greater the potential for specialization.

Determine Job Interrelationships

Once responsibilities are defined, assigned, and grouped by position, establishing a sales management organizational structure is completed by determining job interrelationships. Many configurations are possible. Each agency has its own needs, and the sales manager must choose the configuration that best suits the specific agency. The sales manager must also determine how jobs interrelate and must clearly communicate those relationships to everyone concerned. Sales managers should also define reporting relationships and grant appropriate authority for assigned responsibility, such as binding coverage.

Regardless of the organizational structure, all agency personnel involved should understand that each person is important to the overall success of the sales effort. For example, a producer who does only fact-finding, proposal presentation, and closing should work closely with those employees who obtain the prospects, prepare the proposals, and work with customers as service representatives.

Management Tip—In some agencies, the staff is organized into teams. In an effective team, support staff may be responsible for some production as part of their responsibilities for the team's book of business. The support staff's accountabilities may include the retention percentage on the business they service. These "production CSRs" may eventually develop the skills and knowledge to become producers.

Agency management should communicate the interrelationships among jobs in the agency to their employees. Agency employees should understand how their jobs relate, how they fit into the agency sales management organizational structure, and to whom they report. Inadequate communication of reporting relationships can cause confusion, which can affect productivity and cause dissatisfaction and morale problems. Just as an agency's sales management activities and organizational structure should support the agency's overall business plan, the operations aspects of agency sales management support the agency's sales activities and contribute to the success of the agency's overall business plan.

AGENCY SALES MANAGEMENT OPERATIONS— STAFFING AND PRODUCER HIRING

Part of the operational responsibilities of agency sales management is ensuring that capable and knowledgeable people are in place to support the sales effort and to execute the agency's sales plan so that the agency can meet its strategic goals.

Securing the right people is key to an agency's success. The agency's managers must plan how to staff the agency, make effective hiring decisions, and provide training and development of staff members.

Staffing the Agency

There are four major types of staff in an insurance agency:

- Managers are responsible for meeting the overall goals of the agency. Sales managers are responsible for meeting the agency's sales goals, specifically, answering to the agency owner or principal(s).
- Producers are licensed to sell insurance products and are key to an agency's success in meeting sales objectives.

- Customer service representatives (CSRs) are also licensed and have extensive responsibility in providing service to customers and assisting producers with sales functions.
- Administrative and support staff perform functions that assist managers and key staff members in meeting the agency's goals. The typical functions performed by administrative and support staff include accounting, information technology (IT), human resources (HR), proposal and report preparation, and various other activities.

Small agencies may not have all four types of staff, and large agencies may have various different subtypes of these major categories. Whatever the agency size, management must make effective decisions regarding staffing levels. For example, it must decide whether there will be a full-time sales manager.

The sales manager, along with the agency's other managers, must plan the ratio of producers to CSRs and support staff, and the staffing level required for each type of position. A ratio with a high number of producers to a small number of support staff may result in producers inefficiently spending time on administrative functions. A ratio with a small number of producers to a high level of support staff may result in insufficient resources devoted to selling. To have maximum effectiveness and efficiency to reach sales goals, the ratio of producers to other staff must be the right one for each agency. An agency's managers should plan for current and anticipated business needs in determining staffing ratios.

Agencies should plan their staffing levels on at least an annual basis. As agencies grow and technology continues to change, the management structure as well as the ratio of producers to support staff may need to change to provide optimal effectiveness. For example, an agency that once relied on a full-time receptionist may now use an automated call distribution system, with the former receptionist performing another function, such as customer service or IT. The resources previously expended on this position could be redirected to a new producer position to expand the agency's business.

The agency's managers must also plan the type and amount of compensation for the agency's staff. Producers are typically compensated by a percentage of the commissions they generate. Support staff are typically paid a salary, although some agencies may use a combination of salary and commission for CSRs. Some agencies use bonuses to reward staff for meeting or exceeding sales goals.

Hiring Producers

There are two major reasons for hiring a new producer. The first is to replace a producer who has left the agency. The second is to increase sales for the agency.

When hiring a replacement producer, the hiring manager should determine why the previous producer left and consider the type of producer who should be hired. An exit interview should be conducted with all staff who leave the agency, but especially with producers who leave. Hiring a replacement producer allows managers to expand the agency's business by selecting a candidate who has experience in a different line of insurance or with different insurers or customers. It also offers an opportunity to promote a well-qualified CSR.

An agency's managers may also decide to hire a new producer to increase the agency's sales. Managers should consider the experience desired in the new producer. A growing agency might wish to hire a recent graduate from college or an MBA program who can be trained by the sales manager and/or experienced producers. Alternatively, an agency might wish to hire a producer with an expertise in one or more target market segments, such as construction or management liability, in order to enter or expand into that market.

Managers should plan recruitment efforts toward candidates whose interests, experience, and goals align well with those of the agency. For example, an agency that is experiencing rapid growth because of a growing community may not have the resources available to train an inexperienced producer. Or a producer who specializes in one line of commercial insurance may not have the skills and experience for a small agency that places diverse personal and commercial coverages.

☑ Reality Check

A Successful Agency's Approach to Producer Hiring

A successful family-owned Florida insurance agency hires producers with no property-casualty insurance experience. Rather than hiring recent college graduates, this agency selects candidates with experience in other businesses. It typically selects candidates with backgrounds in life insurance, accounting, or sales who are interested in making a career change.

Elisabeth Boone, "Building a Winning Sales Team," Rough Notes, December 1999, www.roughnotes.com/rnmagazine/search/management/99_12P20.HTM (accessed September 23, 2011). [DA08210]

For an agency to succeed, it must hire the right producers—not only to meet sales goals but also to minimize the time and expense associated with hiring. Advertising for producer positions is usually necessary, and this cost can be significant. If a professional recruiter is used, the cost increases, but the amount of time managers spend in screening and interviewing candidates may decrease. An agency's managers should have a plan in place for hiring producers before a critical need arises.

Developing New and Existing Producers

Because insurance is a dynamic business, ongoing training and education are required for both newly hired producers and existing employees. These are the four major types of educational and training opportunities available for producers and other agency staff:

- Educational organizations—The Institutes offer various educational programs for producers as well as other insurance professionals. In addition to the valued CPCU designation, many other courses, programs, and designations are available. States recognize these courses for continuing education credit. The Institutes also provide custom training programs for clients. The American College offers the Chartered Life Underwriter (CLU) professional designation for professionals in life insurance and related financial services and a Chartered Financial Consultant (ChFC) professional designation program emphasizing financial planning. The College of Financial Planning offers a Certified Financial Planner (CFP) designation. Life Office Management Association (LOMA) is an international association through which many insurance and financial services companies engage in research and educational activities focused on improving company operations.

- Training and continuing education—Producers are required to obtain a certain number of continuing education credits as part of state licensing requirements. Conferences and seminars are provided by professional insurance organizations, such as the CPCU Society. Additionally, organizations such as CEU.com offer training courses to meet these requirements.

- Producer associations—Local, state, and national agents' associations have developed seminars, courses, and workshops to address the training needs of producers in different stages of professional development. For example, both the Independent Insurance Agents and Brokers of America (IIABA) and the National Association of Professional Insurance Agents (PIA) offer their members insurance and management courses.

- Insurers—Some insurers provide formal and informal training for producers at the agencies that represent them. This training may be conducted at classroom locations or at the agency.

An agency's managers need to decide how much training to provide in-house, aside from courses required for licensure. Small agencies may prefer to have an agency manager or senior producer train new producers. Larger agencies may prefer to provide training through an organization that offers a program or customizes training for the agency. Training can be provided online, through self-study texts, in classrooms, or through a combination of these methods.

Regardless of what training methods are used by an agency, producer development must go beyond merely satisfying licensing requirements. Insurance is both complex and dynamic, so producers need to have current knowledge and skills. Also important, for both the individual producer and the agency, is that producers are fully engaged in their profession. Continual professional development can help ensure this engagement.

Apply Your Knowledge

A successful insurance agency is located in a rapidly growing suburban community. The agency has three producers, and one producer is retiring. How many producers should the agency hire?

a. None

b. One

c. Two

d. Requires evaluation

Feedback: d. Careful evaluation by the agency is required to determine how many producers to hire. Because the agency is successful in a growing community, the agency's managers will likely want to replace the retiring producer and may also want to hire one or more additional producers to increase sales and to make the most efficient use of the recruitment and hiring process.

AGENCY SALES MANAGEMENT OPERATIONS— PRODUCER COMPENSATION AND PERFORMANCE

Because producers generate the sales that are necessary for an insurance agency to succeed, it is essential that producers are accountable for meeting sales objectives and that the compensation system reflects producers' performances.

An agency's producer compensation system should be designed to motivate producers to reach sales goals. Sales managers must also actively manage producers' performance to meet the agency's benchmark standards. These are the activities involved in managing producers to achieve sales goals:

* Setting performance standards
* Measuring performance results against those standards
* Using reporting and accountability systems
* Conducting performance evaluations
* Taking corrective action
* Rewarding employees

Compensation Systems

The three most commonly used producer compensation systems are (1) commission only, (2) salary only, and (3) salary and commission.

Generally, the commission-only system works well with experienced producers who have an established book of business. This system may be as simple as applying a fixed percentage of commissions against all business produced. However, many agencies have more intricate systems that pay higher percentages for new business than for renewals, for large than for small renewals (as defined by the agency), and for property-casualty insurance than for life and health and disability insurance. These systems focus the producer's efforts on areas the agency has designated for emphasis or areas that increase agency profitability.

Under the commission-only system, generally 15 to 40 percent of the commissions the agency receives goes to the producer. The amount often depends on how many of the key producer accountabilities the producer performs. The salary-only compensation system is used most commonly with newly hired producers, often for a period of time such as six months or a year. Management determines a salary, which is adjusted quarterly or annually to reflect the producer's sales level.

The salary and commission compensation system is appropriate for a producer who is responsible for producing new business but who still extensively services existing accounts. Salary is paid for servicing renewals, and commission is paid for new business.

Any of these compensation systems may include fringe benefits, such as medical insurance or a retirement plan, as well as extra benefits, such as club memberships, award trips the agency wins from insurers, agency ownership, company automobiles, and expense accounts.

Setting Performance Standards

Agencies can use these performance standards:

- Budgetary standards—The agency's budget can also serve as a performance standard. A well-planned budget gives agency personnel the guidance necessary to meet goals by indicating in financial terms whether the agency plan is being implemented. It is also a sound standard to use for financial comparisons. With a current budget, agency management can easily and quickly evaluate the agency's performance relative to budget projections.

- Sales standards—Individual and agency sales standards, determined by senior management, are integral to planning. They address sales volume, product mix, commission income, and profit levels. These standards then establish the basis for individual performance standards.

- Engineered standards—Engineered standards are based on an objective, quantitative analysis of a specific work situation. They measure the potential output of individual employees or employee groups. For example, some management consultants use the number of premium transactions per administrative employee, which determines, on average, how much work each administrative employee does each working day. A premium transaction is any transaction that produces an invoice, either direct billed or agency billed. An administrative employee is anyone providing internal customer service to other agency staff. By setting an engineered standard such as this, agency management can evaluate how much work is being done and whether the results indicate increasing or decreasing employee performance trends.

- Individual performance standards—Individuals' performance can be compared against their own standards. Performance standards are negotiated with the employees as at the beginning of the evaluation period and documented in writing to support the performance evaluation at the end of the period. Standards should be qualitative (such as positive customer feedback about service provided) and quantitative (such as commissions or numbers of new policies).

- Judgment and experience standards—Most agencies use judgment and experience standards along with the other performance standards in the industry. These standards are not scientific or quantitative; they are based simply on management's judgment and experience. An example of this type of standard is a manager's statement, "I think (I judge) you are doing a good job [based on my experience with your performance as an employee to date]." Usually, quantified standards—for example, those that can be derived from performance evaluations—are needed for comparison purposes to supplement judgment and experience standards.

- Historical standards—Historical standards, such as benchmarks, can come from internal or external sources. Those based on internal sources are most readily available. Using internal standards, the manager can compare the employee's current performance against the agency's past performance. An example of an external standard historical standard is the Insurance Agents and Brokers of America, Inc. (IIABA) *Best Practices* studies. Each IIABA study identifies the top 25 percent of best-performing independent agencies. The annually published findings provide agencies with benchmarks against which to compare their results.

When using the Best Practices information, producers should not be discouraged if they find themselves comparing unfavorably to the standard benchmarks. These agencies and producers providing data on which the practices are set are the top achievers in the industry. The Best Practices study is designed to inspire agencies toward improvement, not to discourage them. See the exhibit "Multi-Line Producer Productivitiy."

Multi-Line Producer Productivitiy

Agency Size (by net revenue)	Average New Commissions	Average Serviced Commissions	Top 25% New Commissions	Top 25% Serviced Commissions
$0–$1,250,000	$37,757	$267,604	$57,519	$498,828
$1,250,000–$2,500,000	$63,611	$409,653	$136,968	$788,656
$2,500,000–$5,000,000	$76,611	$450,559	$138,885	$646,656

Adapted from the 2010 Best Practices Study Update, ©2010 Independent Insurance Agents and Brokers of America, Inc., and Reagan Consulting. [DA08119]

Measuring Performance Results

The performance standards provide the basis for the second activity related to agency control, measuring performance results. Results are measured by comparing the performance standards to actual results. Most agencies measure both overall agency results and individual employee results.

An engineered standard can be applied to an employee's performance to measure efficiency. If the "normal" average number of transactions per employee per day has been determined to be 3.25 by an engineered standard, and if each employee has a transaction count of 6.5, then the employee is operating at a high level of efficiency. This type of standard can be used to evaluate producers' effectiveness in contacting prospects or making calls on existing accounts.

Organizations that create and disseminate external benchmarks can also provide tools for making comparisons. For example, the IIABA *Best Practices* study includes manuals and worksheets available for download, which enable individual agencies to compare their actual results with benchmarks for agencies of similar size.

Using Reporting and Accountability Systems

Reporting systems generated through the agency management system are essential to measuring producer performance. Reports should be generated on a regular basis (weekly, monthly, or quarterly) that show new sales and renewals, commissions generated, prospects added to the database, and other key producer activities.

Budget reports should also be generated and evaluated on a regular basis, and variations from budget expenses should be carefully analyzed. Metrics such as an expense ratio, showing the amount of direct expense and/or time to prospect, sell, or renew an account, might be used.

Conducting Performance Evaluations

Agency managers use the information from performance results comparisons to conduct performance evaluations. It is important for employees to receive regular performance feedback from their manager or supervisor, and they should also have at least one formal evaluation each year.

A common practice in many agencies is to ask the employee to complete a self-evaluation and to use it, along with the evaluation completed by the manager, as the basis for the final evaluation.

The performance evaluation should also serve as the basis for the producer's development plan and as a way to discover changes needed in the agency's program for guiding and training sales personnel. For example, performance evaluations may reveal the need for improvements in technical training necessitated by a regulatory change or the introduction of a new policy form.

Taking Corrective Action

Once performance has been evaluated on the basis of the standards set, the information gathered, and the measurements and comparisons made, the manager takes any necessary corrective action. Corrective action can be taken on an agency-wide or an individual basis. Agency-wide action is required when overall agency goals have not been achieved. Corrective action may involve changes in agency goals, systems, and/or staff. On an individual basis, corrective action is required when an employee is not performing up to the established standards. Such action may involve training, a change in responsibilities, and/or probation or dismissal.

The sales manager should strive to develop all producers to reach the standards of the agency's top producer. The top producer (or producers) should be determined based on several years of performance. Each sales manager should identify the characteristics of the agency's top producers. If other producers fall well short of the top standard, the manager can accompany the producer on prospecting and sales calls and evaluate the producer's performance using the characteristics of the top producer.

Additionally, regular sales meetings can be held where producers are motivated, trained, and coached in successful sales techniques and strategies. It can be helpful to have a top producer conduct some of these meetings or training sessions.

Rewarding Employees

Rewarding producers for meeting or exceeding sales objectives is important. Although financial compensation is the most direct method of reward, it is not the only method. Recognition is also an important form of reward. Some agencies designate top producers with plaques or other visible signs of recognition. Such forms of recognition also serve to motivate other producers.

Additionally, it is also important to reward an entire group or agency for a successful year. Some agencies sponsor trips for groups of producers who meet or exceed goals. Such trips not only reward the producers and provide a few days of relaxation after a busy season, but also can increase camaraderie and therefore cooperation among the producer staff. Celebrations that include all of the agency's staff, such as an annual picnic or dinner, can provide appropriate forums to recognize outstanding performance of the entire agency as well as individuals.

AGENCY SALES MANAGEMENT CASE STUDY

Knowing how to apply the principles of sales management to the facts of a case is an important skill. By carefully considering the facts provided and answering the Knowledge to Action questions, this activity should help you make the transition from knowing sales management concepts to knowing how to apply those concepts in the context of a hypothetical sales meeting.

Case Facts

Allison is the new sales manager at Inkto Insurance Agency. She schedules an all-day meeting with the agency's producers to discuss the agency's goals. After meeting with the agency's owners, Allison plans to use the bottom-up approach to sales planning, and she will use this meeting to obtain input from the producers on sales targets that align with the overall goals of the agency. The agency owners' goals are retention of 95 percent of current accounts and growth of 20 percent in new commissions.

For the prior year, each experienced personal lines producer had a sales objective of $30,000 in new commissions, while new personal lines producers had a sales objective of $10,000 in new commissions. All of the commercial lines producers were experienced, and their sales objective was $50,000 each in new commissions. By a slight margin, more of the agency's growth of 15 percent in the prior year was achieved in personal lines than commercial lines.

Allison will discuss with the producers how they plan to achieve the agency's growth goal. Before this discussion, Allison will present the agency's new relationship with Ultimate Insurance Co. Ultimate, a commercial lines insurer, is adding Inkto as one of its preferred agencies. In addition to offering a preferred commission rate for meeting business placement targets, Ultimate is also offering marketing assistance.

After discussion of sales objectives, Allison will discuss the agency's organizational structure. Inkto's current structure has a group of customer service representatives (CSRs) who are aligned with either personal lines or commercial lines. Allison will propose aligning CSRs with each carrier the agency represents.

The meeting will be held in a new conference room that features technology for remote attendees to participate. Two of the producers will participate in the meeting remotely. Allison will discuss the agency's mobile technology, through which producers can obtain real-time quotes from carriers on their cellular phones.

At the conclusion of the meeting, Allison will discuss producer development opportunities.

When answering the questions in this case-based activity, consider only the information supported by the facts of the case and any recommended tools.

Case Analysis Tools

The bottom-up sales management approach involves an agency's producers in setting sales targets and objectives to meet an agency's sales goals. The agency's organizational structure, technology, performance and compensation system, and producer development should all be developed and aligned with the agency's overall strategic goals.

Overview of Steps

Allison prepares this agenda for the meeting with the producers:

* Introduction of the agency's overall goals
* Presentation of the new carrier relationship
* Discussion of sales objectives
* Discussion of the agency's organizational structure
* Presentation of new mobile technology
* Producer development opportunities

Introduction of the Agency's Overall Goals

Allison understands that producers have prepared for this meeting by reviewing their individual books of business and developing preliminary sales plans for the coming year. Because there is not much growth in the region's economy, she anticipates that some negotiation may occur with the producers on reaching the agency's overall goals. However, she is hopeful that by including the producers in setting objectives, they will be able to reach the desired goals.

Knowledge to Action

In a bottom-up sales management approach, how should Allison present the agency's goals at the start of the producer meeting?

a.   "The agency's owners and I have set the sales goals for the year."

b.   "The agency's owners expect all producers to meet the agency's sales goals."

c.   "The agency's owners have a goal for the agency and would like your input on how to reach it."

d.   "I am going to set individual sales goals so that my department will meet the agency's overall sales goal."

Feedback: c. In a bottom-up sales management approach, the manager seeks input from producers on setting sales goals and objectives that will meet the agency's overall goals. Although producers are expected to meet sales goals, it is important first to include the producers in setting the goals in a bottom-up approach.

Presentation of the New Carrier Relationship

The new carrier's target commercial market is the small to mid-size market, and this creates a good fit for Inkto. Ultimate is focused on providing extensive customer service, and this also aligns well with Inkto's philosophy. Ultimate wants to aggressively market in Inkto's region, and the carrier's production goals for new business should provide momentum for Inkto's sales.

Knowledge to Action

Why is it important for Allison to present the new carrier relationship before discussing sales goals and objectives with the producers? Select all that apply.

a.   The new relationship offers new commission-growth opportunities.

b.   The new relationship offers marketing assistance.

c.   The new relationship offers assistance to producers in meeting goals.

d.   The new relationship makes it unnecessary to set sales objectives.

Feedback: a, b, and c. The new carrier relationship will offer new commission-growth opportunities and marketing assistance. This new offering will affect how the producers develop sales objectives. However, it will not make it unnecessary to set those objectives, which will include business placed with other carriers.

Discussion of Sales Objectives

With the addition of the new carrier, Allison anticipates a great deal of discussion regarding the sales objectives for commercial and personal lines.

Knowledge to Action

Which one of the following would the producers at the meeting be most likely to recommend?

a. Higher commission goals for personal lines producers
b. Same goals for both personal lines and commercial lines producers
c. Higher commission goals for commercial lines producers

Feedback: c. Because of the new relationship with a commercial lines insurer, the producers are more likely to recommend higher commission goals for the commercial lines producers.

Would the producers at the meeting be likely to advocate a similar ratio as last year between personal lines and commercial lines for this year's 20 percent growth target?

a. Yes
b. No

Feedback: b. Because Ultimate is a commercial lines carrier, the producers are likely to recommend a commercial lines growth target that is slightly greater than the personal lines target for this year's objectives.

Discussion of the Agency's Organizational Structure

Allison has discussed the agency's sales organizational structure with the owners. She is not certain that the current structure is the most effective approach, and she looks forward to discussing this with the producers.

Knowledge to Action

What is an advantage of aligning CSRs with carriers represented by the agency? Select all that apply.

a.   Each CSR will become expert in a carrier system.

b.   CSRs will be better able to explain policy provisions to customers.

c.   CSRs will develop a better rapport with individual producers.

Feedback: a. and b. If CSRs are aligned with insurance carriers, they will become expert in those carriers' systems and policies, and therefore be better able to explain the provisions of those carriers' policies to customers. However, unless the producers are similarly aligned, there would not be any expected increase in CSRs' rapport with producers.

A majority of the producers at the meeting prefer aligning CSRs by customer/account rather than by carrier. What is an advantage of this organizational structure? Select all that apply.

a.   CSRs will become more knowledgeable about customer needs.

b.   CSRs will develop a greater rapport with customers.

c.   CSRs will develop a greater rapport with producers.

d.   CSRs will increase their efficiency significantly.

Feedback: a, b, and c. CSRs are likely to be more knowledgeable about customer needs and develop a greater rapport with customers if they are aligned by customer in the organizational structure. They are also likely to develop a greater rapport with producers who will be responsible for certain accounts. However, there would not necessarily be a significant increase in efficiency in this structure.

To what goal would aligning CSRs by customer/account contribute?

a.   Increasing new commissions

b.   Achieving retention

c.   Both new commissions and retention

Feedback: b. The increase in customer rapport and knowledge of customer needs would be likely to contribute toward the retention goal.

Presentation of New Mobile Technology

The new agency technology will provide more mobile capabilities for producers. They will be able to obtain quotes, market comparisons, and other information from mobile telephones. Sales presentations can be loaded onto producers' laptops.

Knowledge to Action

Why is mobile technology important to producers and their agency? Select all that apply.

a. Mobile technology can provide solutions while producers are meeting with clients.

b. Mobile technology can allow producers to work remotely.

c. Mobile technology can decrease commuting and other travel time.

d. Mobile technology is a current trend.

Feedback: a, b, and c. Mobile technology is increasingly important to insurance agencies and producers. New technology solutions offer improved communications between producers, who are frequently out of the office on sales calls, and their agency. Additionally, capabilities are available to provide data, quotations, regulatory updates, and claim information on mobile technology platforms. However, it may not be practical for an agency to purchase mobile technology simply because it is a current trend. The technology should be evaluated and purchased according to the needs of the agency and its producers.

Producer Development Opportunities

Allison asks for recommendations from the producers for development opportunities that go beyond merely providing required continuing education credits.

Knowledge to Action

What should producers recommend? Select all that apply.

a. An insurance industry professional designation, such as CPCU

b. Producer conferences at which educational seminars are presented

c. General insurance industry conferences at which producers can network and obtain education

d. Undergraduate or graduate programs in insurance and risk management

Feedback: a, b, c, and d. All of these options present development opportunities beyond merely completing courses required to maintain producer licenses. The type of development program chosen should reflect the goals of both the individual producer and the agency. For example, a producer who has not completed an undergraduate degree may best serve both individual and agency goals by working toward the degree. Therefore, a top commercial lines producer may benefit most from attending a conference with opportunities to network with insurers and potential clients.

SUMMARY

Sales management is the planning, leading, organizing, and controlling of sales efforts to achieve organizational goals. Managing an agency's sales and operations directly influences an organization's effectiveness. It affects the sales management purposes, systems, process, and organizational structure. Two purposes of agency sales management are to maximize the agency's production efforts and to promote agency effectiveness.

Agency sales management systems can be either top-down or bottom-up. In a top-down system, management determines the long-range and annual sales goals for the agency and how those goals will be achieved. In a bottom-up system, producers or branch offices participate in setting sales goals. To be successful, either system requires appropriate technological support and a consensus between producers and management.

The steps in the sales management process mirror the organizational planning process. They ensure that the sales manager develops a mission statement, goals, strategies, objectives, and budgets; establishes policies and procedures; and monitors the plan, all of which support the agency's overall plan.

The three steps involved in establishing a sales management organizational structure are to (1) define and assign responsibilities, (2) group responsibilities by position, and (3) determine job interrelationships.

For an insurance agency to meet its goals and objectives, it must determine the type and level of staff required. Producers are the key sales staff, and managers should carefully evaluate prospective producers' experience and backgrounds to meet the agency's business needs. In addition to training that is required for licensing, agencies should provide both initial and ongoing development of producers to help both the individual producer and the agency succeed.

Agency managers align compensation systems with producers' sales results. Sales managers accomplish agency sales goals by setting producer performance standards, measuring results, using reporting systems, conducting performance evaluations, taking corrective action, and rewarding employees.

It is important for agency sales meetings to contribute to the effectiveness of producers in meeting the agency's goals. In a bottom-up sales management approach, a meeting at which managers discuss overall goals with producers is a key component of obtaining producers' input on sales targets and objectives.

Direct Your Learning ▶▶

Personal Production Plans

Educational Objectives

After learning the content of this assignment, you should be able to:

▷ Explain how the various steps in the personal production planning process enable a producer to achieve specific goals that are consistent with the agency's overall strategic objectives.

▷ Explain how a personal production plan supports the agency's strategic goals and how an agency uses a personal production plans summary.

▷ Describe five strategies producers use to manage time effectively.

▷ Describe the negotiating rules and techniques that are important in principled negotiating and how they can result in a "win-win" scenario.

▷ Given a scenario regarding an insurance agency, demonstrate how a producer, using a well-designed personal production plan and good time management, is able to negotiate a "win-win" resolution on an account.

Personal Production Plans

PERSONAL PRODUCTION PLAN PROCESS

Because selling is the most important part of a producer's job, producers must thoroughly understand how to create plans that describe what they will sell, how much they will sell, and how they will accomplish their sales goals.

A **personal production plan** must be consistent with and support an agency's plans. It also should be as detailed as an agency's plan; therefore, it is developed using the same seven steps:

1. Develop a mission statement.
2. Develop goals.
3. Develop strategies.
4. Develop objectives.
5. Determine budgets.
6. Establish policies and procedures.
7. Monitor the plan.

A producer can be held accountable to the plan he or she has created. Agency management system software allows producers to see immediately the results of their efforts, to demonstrate accountability to the plan, and to ensure that goals are aligned throughout the organization.

An agency can combine and summarize individual production plans. If the agency uses bottom-up planning, the resulting summary provides agency sales projections; if the agency uses top-down planning, the resulting summary serves as a basis for planning that can be revised based on management's requirements.

Develop a Mission Statement

A producer sells insurance products suited to the needs of customers; therefore, the first step in creating a personal production plan is to develop a mission statement that addresses those needs. A personal mission statement

> **Personal production plan**
> A written document developed by a producer that describes what the producer will accomplish, how it will be accomplished, and when it will be accomplished.

should align with the agency's corporate mission statement. These are examples of personal mission statements:

- "To serve the financial services needs of the community"
- "To find those people or organizations I can serve within the provisions of my agency contract"
- "To provide premier risk management services to my community"

Develop Goals

Goals are producers' final targets for the planning period. The typical production (or sales) planning period is one year and should coincide with the agency's fiscal year. For example, if an agency operates on a January 1 to December 31 calendar year, then the producer's plan should cover the same period. See the exhibit "SMART Goals."

Producers should establish goals in every area of their accountabilities and developmental activities. For example, in addition to production goals, producers should have goals for professional development and training, income, supervision, and any other area in which they want to make significant progress. By clearly establishing goals and showing the relative priorities among them, producers can effectively allocate their time. See the exhibit "Goal Assessment."

Develop Strategies

Once goals have been set, strategies can be developed to indicate specific ways the producers can achieve their goals and, ultimately, their missions.

Using the mission statement "To serve the financial services needs of the community" as an example, a producer can develop several hypothetical strategies:

- To provide total risk management services for small businesses and not-for-profit organizations
- To serve the life insurance, health insurance, and employee benefit needs of for-profit and not-for-profit organizations
- To develop technical competence within my agency in insurance for trucks, yachts, marinas, and laundries

These three hypothetical strategies are personal, relate to the organization's mission and goals, and narrow the focus of personal activities; yet they remain broad enough to allow a variety of sales activities.

Strategies should identify specific markets for current selling activities, and a marketing strategy should be developed if the producer wants to expand the number of markets addressed within the next few planning periods. Finally, strategies should be shared so that others in the agency can coordinate

SMART Goals

Like agency goals, personal goals should be specific, measurable, achievable, relevant, and time bound (SMART):

Specific—Specifically stated goals clearly tell support staff what is expected of them and help managers better design performance standards and reporting systems. For instance, a producer's goal may be, "I will sell $100,000 of homeowners insurance." But this goal is ambiguous. The producer's sales manager will have no idea whether the $100,000 refers to annualized premiums sold, annualized commission income, or homeowners dwelling coverage.

Measurable—A producer's goal must be measurable, or quantifiable, to determine whether it has been accomplished. A goal that reads, "I will sell more commercial insurance," is not quantifiable because the producer did not specify how much "more" is. To be measurable, the goal could read, "I will generate 15 percent more annualized premiums for commercial property insurance than I did the last plan year." Some goals, such as service goals, may not seem measurable, but can be quantified through customer satisfaction surveys or retention rates. Agency management system reporting can measure progress toward a goal in the terms defined by the producer and the sales manager.

Achievable—A producer's goals must be achievable. The goal, "Every week, I will contact 300 prospects with x-dates during 20X1," is unachievable. A goal that states, "Each week I will telephone ten prospects that I requested from my customers," is achievable—provided that the producer actually contacts customers to request referrals.

Relevant—The agency principal or sales manager and the producer determine whether a goal is relevant in relation to other producer and agency goals. For example, if a producer annually generates $25,000 in commissions from referrals alone, a goal that states, "I will generate $40,000 in commissions from referrals between December 1, 20X1, and December 1, 20X2," is clearly a relevant goal. However, the goal, "I will spend 25 percent of my time per week cold-calling prospects," is probably not a relevant sales goal, particularly when the producer's abilities and time are better spent on more profitable referral business.

Time Bound—For each goal, the producer must include a specific time for completion. A personal production goal should be written so that the timeline is clear to all. Goals should indicate specific completion dates rather than use general terms such as "this year" or "in this period." For example, "I will sell five automobile dealer accounts this year" becomes time bound when restated to read, "I will sell five new automobile dealer accounts by June 30, 20X1." The revised goal clearly specifies when the target must be met. Problems can arise when the deadline extends beyond the planning period. In such cases, the producer should establish interim milestones that indicate substantial progress toward the final goal.

[DA08120]

<hr>

Goal Assessment

Consider whether these examples of supervision and production goals have the characteristics required of SMART goals:

Supervision Goal: "During 200X, I will cross-train the staff in my department."

This goal is neither specific nor measurable. Cross-training means that one person learns the duties and responsibilities of another person within the department. But it is not clear which duties and activities will be part of the cross-training. Should everyone in the department be able to handle all or just a portion of someone else's job? Goal achievement cannot be measured without specifics. The goal is, however, time bound, relevant, and achievable.

Production Goal: "During calendar year 20X1, I will generate $5,000 of new personal lines revenue other than life insurance."

This goal is specific and measurable. Each personal lines product will be included, except life insurance. Homeowners, auto, personal umbrella, recreational vehicles, and mobile homeowners all qualify. Premium volume can be measured. Using a commission or policy count would also be an appropriate measure. The goal is time bound because it is to be met during the calendar year 20X1. It appears relevant to both the producer and the agency. And it appears achievable if other goals do not take too much of the producer's time and energy to accomplish.

<hr>

[DA08121]

activities. See the exhibit "The Planning Process and Its Development Through Various Planning Applications."

Develop Objectives

Objectives are milestones toward goals and should be directed at accomplishing the goals they support. Like goals, objectives should be specific, measurable, time bound, achievable, and relevant. When developing goals and objectives, the producer should first list each goal and then specify the objectives that support it. See the exhibit "Education Goals and Objectives for Joan Producer."

The cross-training goal reads: "By the end of 200X, each of the three support people in my department will be able to handle the duties of the others." The intent is to operate the department efficiently in the absence of any one member, and the producer has until the end of the year to accomplish the cross-training. The producer should then determine what activities must be performed by the deadline to accomplish the goal. Such activities form the basis of the objectives.

The Planning Process and Its Development Through Various Planning Applications

The steps in the planning process allow an agency to develop plans for action. Agency management system software can allow an agency to develop templates for its producers' personal production plans that align them with the agency's overall strategy. Here are some examples of how goals develop through the organizational, agency, and individual producer levels:

Develop a Mission Statement

Organizational management—To serve the financial services needs of the Philadelphia community.

Agency sales management—To provide superior risk management and insurance services products to the tri-state area.

Personal production plans—To provide premier insurance products and risk management services to my customers.

Develop Goals

Organizational management—Our organization will select two insurance brokerages with which to cross-sell $3,000,000 of financial services products within the next twenty-four months.

Agency sales management—Our agency will represent only insurers assigned a key rating of A+ or higher on A.M. Best's Financial Strength Rating Scale.

Personal production plans—In calendar year 200X, I will generate $50,000 in financial services commissions by cross-selling such products to my new property-casualty customers booked within the same period.

Develop Strategies

Organizational management—Our organization will form a strategic partnership with one super-regional insurance brokerage and will merge with one local insurance brokerage.

Agency sales management—Producers will develop production plans targeting new business that will not have to be marketed, except in rare cases, to excess and surplus lines markets.

Personal production plans—I will develop a new business marketing plan targeting not-for-profit, educational, and professional institutions.

[DA08122]

Develop Budgets

Budgets are usually allocated in units of money but can also be expressed in terms of other resource units, such as time. Producers should consider how to budget both money and time as part of their personal planning. Although agencies usually support producers financially in their sales activities, a specific individual sales activity may not be included in the agency's overall sales and advertising budget. A producer should include the estimated time for such an activity in his or her plan. For example, if a producer participates as a sponsor at a commercial account's annual charity golf event, the producer's budget plan should include the related expenses.

Education Goals and Objectives for Joan Producer

1. I will complete a property insurance educational course by June 200X.

- I will find a property insurance course to take by January 31, 200X.

- I will register for the course by March 31, 200X.

- I will buy myself a reward by August 200X if I complete the course as planned.

2. I will teach a general insurance class for my office staff during 200X–0Y.

- I will hold classes once a week for fifteen weeks (this includes two review sessions) during the stated period.

- I will actively solicit participation within the office six weeks before the beginning of classes.

- I will begin the class no later than October 1, 200X.

- I will spend two hours each Saturday preparing for the class.

- I will treat each student who attends thirteen of fifteen classes to lunch.

[DA08123]

Time budgeting is the allocation of available business-related time toward the accomplishment of the producer's goals. Producers should estimate the time necessary to complete all activities included in their plans, such as making a certain number of x-date telephone calls, prospecting appointments, and proposals.

Establish Policies and Procedures

Policies are guidelines for making decisions and performing activities. For example, a producer may have as a policy, "Any agency-billed accounts that are fifteen days past due on premium payment will be sent notice of cancellation. Any exceptions must be approved by management." This policy, if communicated to the support staff who process and mail the necessary paperwork, limits staff to a single course of action in most cases.

Whereas policies indicate what should be done, procedures indicate how things should be done. For instance, as part of the personal plan, the producer may decide to use an introductory mailing program. A procedure could be established for support staff to periodically create and mail solicitation letters to a selected number of automobile dealers.

Monitor the Plan

Plans should be monitored throughout the plan period, tracking activity against goals and objectives. Agencies have several approaches to monitoring plans, including self-monitoring by producers and monitoring by the agency principal or sales manager at weekly, monthly, or quarterly sales meetings.

Using agency management systems or production-tracking software programs, producer and agency results can be measured against goals and objectives on a daily, weekly, monthly, quarterly, or annual basis, tailoring reports to individual agency needs. These are examples of information that such reports may contain:

- Annual net commission goals
- Number of referrals received
- Number of cross-selling referrals obtained
- Number of x-dates obtained
- Number of successful contacts made
- Number of quotes issued
- Number of new policy sales
- Number of lost policies
- Annual net commissions lost

Regardless of which monitoring method is used, producers are ultimately accountable for achieving their annual production plan goals and objectives. Producers who achieve their goals enable agencies to achieve their goals. Therefore, agency principals and sales managers usually are willing to assist producers in making plan adjustments if doing so improves a producer's chances for success.

PERSONAL PRODUCTION PLANS SUMMARY

Individual producer plans are the building blocks of an agency's annual sales production plans. Many agencies combine all their producers' personal production plans into a personal production plans summary.

An agency production plans summary provides an overview of all of the producers' goals, which should support the agency's goals and mission. Agencies should share this summary with all agency personnel, including claim, technology, and support staff, who assist producers in achieving annual production goals. A producer's annual production goal is supported by underlying annual objectives and key production activities, which are monitored monthly. The annual production goal also includes a monthly activity analysis, with a calculation for the number of quotes and accounts written that the producer needs to achieve the annual goal. See the exhibit "XYZ Agency—Personal Producer Production Plan (Partial Plan)."

XYZ Agency—Personal Producer Production Plan (Partial Plan)

Annual Production Goal

Increase annual production by 25 percent net commissions to support XYZ agency goal.

Annual Objectives

a.   Request referrals from all current customers and new customers.

b.   Generate 250 cross-selling opportunities (life, health, financial services, collaborating with other producers).

c.   Obtain 800 personal lines x-dates.

d.   Obtain 600 commercial lines x-dates.

e.   Maintain retention level of current book of business at 97 percent.

f.   Increase hit ratio by 5 percent on personal lines and commercial lines sales.

Key Production Activities—Monitored Monthly

a.   Generate referrals—Generate a database either from current and new customer contacts or via networking, trade association contacts, and so on.

b.   Cross-sell—Generate a minimum of 20 opportunities per month. Start with current customers and collaborate with other producers or other key business leaders in the geographic area.

c.   Obtain personal lines x-dates—Obtain minimum of 67 per month. Mine the agency's current customer database and request the agency principal to hire a part-time telemarketer to generate leads/x-dates. Consider collaborating with other producers to budget for this service.

d.   Obtain commercial insurance x-dates—Obtain 50 per month. Mine the agency's current customer database and same as (c) above. Additionally, pay the telemarketer an additional fee for every "booked" producer appointment in addition to an x-date for commercial lines accounts.

e.   Maintain retention level—Begin working on renewal business 90-120 days before policy expiration dates. Reserve desired insurer markets well in advance if remarketing of accounts may be required. Provide excellent year-round service; use CSRs to handle routine service matters when applicable.

f.   Increase hit ratio—Ensure that all accounts submitted for quoting are prequalified by submitting new business applicants to the agency sales manager for review prior to quoting. If accounts do not meet target markets of agency's insurers, or if the agency has little expertise in handling certain accounts, do not waste time "practice-quoting."

Monthly Activity Analysis

a.   Net annual renewal commissions expected (including rate changes, 97 percent retention) — $100,000

b.   Total annual production goal — $125,000

c.   Annual total sales goal needed (subtract item 1 from item 2) — $25,000

d.   Annual total new customers (divide item 3 by average customer commission per account – $300) — 83

e.   Number of annual quotes needed (divide item 4 by expected hit ratio of 30 percent) — 277

Tracking

Monthly quotes _____ Monthly accounts written _____ Monthly net commissions _____

[DA08076]

When producers work with sales managers in finalizing their personal production plans, they should consider certain characteristics of production plans that often prove to be successful. A model personal production plan for a producer should possess these five characteristics:

- The producer's personal production plan should be negotiated with the sales manager or principal to ensure that producers direct their efforts towards the type of business the agency wants to sell. In addition, the producer's plan may require assistance from members of the agency staff who report to the sales manager.

- A model personal production plan gives a producer a set of self-directed sales activities that are derived from and support the goals and objectives. Independent, entrepreneurial activities encourage the producer to focus on executing the production plan. For example, producers may be involved in cross-selling and networking, referral and lead generation, and prospecting activities, all of which are self-directed.

- A negotiated personal production plan with specific goals and objectives gives the sales manager or agency principal a convenient evaluation tool. If a producer is not meeting a particular sales goal, the sales manager and producer can review the objectives. It may become obvious that the goal itself is unrealistic and that sales efforts would be better directed toward another target market. In such a case, the sales manager and producer can negotiate new goals. In other cases, achieving the goal may be easy because the objectives were effective. The agency may share these effective objectives with other producers to improve their performance.

- An agency that negotiates a personal production plan and assists the producer with meeting goals and objectives helps the producer generate new business more rapidly. The producer may take less time than otherwise to become productive, contributing to the agency's profits more quickly and reducing the time and money invested in the producer. The sales manager can use a negotiated personal production plan to check on the producer's progress. In some cases this practice enables the sales manager or principal to recognize a mismatch between the individual and the job much earlier than otherwise, saving the agency both time and money.

- The producer must formulate a personal production plan corresponding with the agency's plan. Insurer representation determines the size and types of business the agency can produce. If the agency emphasizes commercial lines over personal lines, property-casualty insurance over life and health insurance, and large over small accounts, the producer's goals must do the same. If the producer has one set of goals and the agency has another, neither will meet its goals.

When preparing production plans, producers should consider the benefits of referrals as a new-business source. If consistently obtained, referrals can develop into one of an agency's top sources of new business customers.

TIME MANAGEMENT

Time is one of the producer's most valuable resources. Time management can help producers focus on fulfilling their personal production plans, which focus on sales.

As a practical matter, producers spend most of their time servicing existing customers and managing their accounts, leaving little time available for selling. One estimate is that producers spend less than one hour of selling for every four hours of nonselling time. Producers can use these five essential time management strategies to increase the time available for selling:

- Eliminate time-wasters
- Set priorities
- Prepare for meetings
- Plan
- Manage phone calls and e-mails

Eliminate Time-Wasters

For one of his books on time management, *The Time Trap*, R. Alec Mackenzie, a renowned time management expert, conducted research with businesspeople around the world, including insurance agents. Based on that research, Mackenzie devised a list of twenty major time-wasters that interfere with people's achieving their goals, listed in order of importance:[1]

1. Management by crisis
2. Telephone interruptions
3. Inadequate planning
4. Attempting too much
5. Drop-in visitors
6. Ineffective delegation
7. Personal disorganization
8. Lack of self-discipline
9. Inability to say "no"
10. Procrastination
11. Meetings
12. Paperwork
13. Leaving tasks unfinished
14. Inadequate staff
15. Socializing
16. Confused responsibility or authority
17. Poor communication
18. Inadequate controls and progress reports

19. Incomplete information
20. Travel

Producers who establish and adhere to a sales system with a personal production plan can mitigate the effects of many time-wasters. For example, Mackenzie refers to management by crisis, which he defines as "dealing with a crisis after it occurs." One way to avoid a crisis situation is by planning for the best way to keep it from occurring—such as, for insurance producers, ensuring that customers who require flood coverage are offered flood insurance well before any threat of hurricane occurs.

To minimize telephone interruptions, the producer can use technology or seek the cooperation of other staff to determine priorities and screen telephone calls. Important customer calls and emergency calls should be handled immediately. Other calls can be referred to support staff, postponed, or expedited within predetermined guidelines.

The exhibit provides other practical suggestions to help producers eliminate the time-wasters listed. Some of the techniques can address several different timewasters. Information on time management is available from many sources, and the illustrations provided in this exhibit are not meant to be comprehensive. See the exhibit "Eliminating Time-Wasters."

Set Priorities

Setting and adhering to priorities are the heart of an effective time management system. As with goals and objectives, failing to establish priorities makes it easy to ignore them or to let other activities get in their way.

Many time management systems recommend setting priorities. They suggest starting by listing every task that needs to be done in a given amount of time. A letter (or number) is then assigned to each task, establishing its relative importance. Some systems use three levels of priorities; others use four or five. The system a producer chooses is not as important as the process itself.

For example, four priority levels for tasks may be used, labeled as priorities A through D:

1. Important and urgent (As)
2. Important but not urgent (Bs)
3. Urgent but not important (Cs)
4. Not important and not urgent (Ds)

Key to any time management system is defining the terms "important" and "urgent." The focus for producers must be on what is important. An important task can be defined as any task that leads to accomplishing goals. An urgent task is one that demands immediate action. Once the importance of tasks has been identified, they can be separated into those that are and those that are not urgent and labeled A, B, C, or D.

Eliminating Time-Wasters

Management by Crisis

- Set and adhere to deadlines to avoid self-created crises.

- Build extra time into schedules to handle unanticipated events.

- Conduct an after-action review after each crisis to determine how to avoid or better manage future crises.

Telephone and E-Mail Interruptions

- Forward phone calls to support staff or voice mail during certain periods to allow blocks of uninterrupted time.

- Set aside certain times when you routinely ask people to call.

- Designate blocks of time for returning phone calls and e-mails.

- Create a voice-mail message requesting that callers leave all information necessary to respond to the call.

Inadequate Planning

- List long-term goals and specify associated short-term goals or objectives with intermediate dates.

- End each day by determining what you will accomplish the next day.

Attempting Too Much

- Break large tasks into a series of small tasks.

- Complete one task before you begin another.

Ineffective Delegation

- Make a list of recurring tasks; determine which tasks are delegable to other staff members, and make assignments.

- Determine which tasks other staff members could complete after training; arrange for required training.

- Conduct a staff audit to determine who is doing what, who needs additional skills, and whose responsibilities can be expanded.

Personal Disorganization

- Group similar tasks and perform them at the same time.

- Take advantage of the agency management system software's organizational tools.

- Work on tasks for one project at a time.

Lack of Self-Discipline; Procrastination

- Select the top two or three tasks daily from your "To Do" list that are important and urgent and that you dislike doing. Complete these tasks first to avoid being distracted by them throughout the day.

- Complete the hardest task(s) for the day first.

Inability to Say "No"

- Select and rehearse a standard phrase you can use when asked to do something that is not your responsibility. For example, "I can understand how you need help with this project. However, my projects are consuming all of my time."

Meetings

- Determine whether a meeting really is necessary.
- Set goals, agendas, and time limits for all meetings.
- Set aside particular times of the week for all meetings.
- Start and end meetings on time.

Leaving Tasks Unfinished

- Estimate the amount of time needed to complete a task; schedule sufficient time to complete each task; work on one task at a time to the exclusion of all others.
- Maintain a running list of next tasks to be performed in all project folders; check off each task as completed.

Socializing

- For a week or two, track the amount of work time you spend socializing, with whom, and where; estimate how much work time you are losing each year; avoid persons and situations that cause you to over-socialize at work.

Confused Responsibility or Authority

- Clarify job responsibility and authority with supervisor and any direct reports at the beginning of each performance year and new project.

Poor Communication

- Identify who needs to be notified of what for each task.

Inadequate Controls and Progress Reports

- Develop formal procedures for complex but routine tasks.
- Create checklists to ensure that processes are correctly followed.
- Create an electronic template for progress reports, indicating required information.

Incomplete Information

- Specify the information that meeting attendees will need to bring to a meeting, or provide it in advance.

Travel

- Combine several visits per trip.
- Set aside specific times of the month or year for business travel to minimize work disruptions at other times.
- Create an action plan for each business trip, and strive to complete the plan on each trip to minimize follow-up travel.

[DA08088]

Urgent tasks are typically time sensitive and often involve demands on a producer's time made by colleagues or customers. However, urgent items may or may not be the most important tasks the producer should complete to achieve his or her goal. For example, a producer receiving a last-minute call to attend a new business meeting with a prospect he has long pursued would classify the task as important and urgent (A). However, if the producer is interrupted on his way out by one of his fellow producers, who requests his help to complete one of the agency's new production forms, this task can be classified as urgent but not important (C) because it does not help the first producer move toward achieving his goals.

Both A and B tasks are important. The difference is the sense of urgency and immediacy of an A task. However, constantly working only on tasks labeled "urgent" leads to what has been called the "tyranny of the urgent," treating priorities as if all plans, goals, and objectives should be developed, implemented, and accomplished in one day. Because plans actually cover months, a short-term focus on A tasks can lead to stress, burnout, and eventual failure.

Management author Stephen Covey, in *The 7 Habits of Highly Effective People*, calls the practice of changing the focus from handling only the current emergency to spending time preparing for future needs "sharpening the saw."[2] The analogy is clear—one who spends all his or her time on emergencies may accomplish work, but at some point the person, like the saw, is going to become worn down and useless. Some time must be spent "sharpening the saw" by completing tasks involving learning, reflecting, and planning. In fact, Covey suggests spending the most time doing B items.

For producers, B tasks such as training and education prepare them for opportunities that may occur farther along in planning periods. For example, training and education can enhance a producer's ability to serve customers and prospects in the future. Prospects can become next year's customers. For B tasks, producers should think in terms of investing for a long-term payoff.

A producer can increase the amount and effectiveness of time spent on A and B tasks by concentrating on selling activities during the time of day he or she feels most alert and works most efficiently that is, peak performance times.

Marketing Tip—Taking the long-term view of priorities can be difficult, particularly for new producers who are trying to build their business. They may overpromise or give up too much just to get the sale. As a result, the agency and the producer may later lose money on the account or incur an E&O claim. A new producer concentrating on making the present sale may not consider such future results. Producers should understand that every action has a consequence. Today's quick sale may lead to tomorrow's unsatisfied customer and a loss of referral business.

Prepare for Meetings

Meetings can consume substantial time; therefore, preparation for meetings with customers is another time-management strategy. Producers should have a specific goal in mind before any meeting. For example, if the purpose of a meeting is to obtain an x-date, every effort should be made to obtain the date and, once obtained, to end the meeting. Without a goal, a meeting can extend past its usefulness. Producers should arrive at a customer meeting with all the information and materials required to respond to the customers' inquiries and to accomplish the goal.

In any sales call, producers should know the essential points to make. A short outline of why a producer wants a customer's or prospect's policy expiration dates can help to organize the call. If the goal of an appointment is to present technical suggestions about coverage changes or risk management procedures designed to minimize premiums, the producer should arrange the suggestions and arguments logically beforehand. Such preparation contributes to an organized, effective sales presentation.

Marketing Tip—A good way to prepare for an important presentation is to try it out on a member of the agency staff, preferably a nontechnical person. In this way, the producer not only gets practice but also receives feedback about clarity and persuasiveness. A technical person may overlook the producer's repeated use of insurance terms (such as "UM" and "comp" for uninsured motorist and workers' compensation coverage) that a prospect may not understand. A nontechnical person can point out when the terms used are vague or confusing, so that the producer can translate insurance language into the prospect's language.

When making an appointment, the producer should set an end time as well as a start time and should inform the customer of both times. Whereas time is a producer's most valuable resource, it is also important to the customer. Promptness is important. When budgeting for travel time, producers should allow for delays by considering time of day, particularly when traveling long distances or through congested areas.

Producers can also use meal times for appointments or meetings. A common practice in many areas is to begin the day with a breakfast appointment. A nonworking lunch for many is essentially a C task. However, it can become an A or a B task if combined with a sales-related appointment.

Plan

Another time management strategy is to plan. One ongoing planning method is to plan the next day or week at the end of the current day or week. Precise allocations of time are not necessary, but reviewing what needs to be done the next day or the next week helps the producer allocate time effectively. The time allocated should be appropriate for the task. For instance, allocating three hours to acquire a personal auto policy x-date is excessive. Three hours may be inadequate, however, to complete a commercial insurance loss exposure analysis.

Manage Phone Calls and E-Mail

One of the most challenging time management issues for producers is how to manage phone calls and e-mail. Cell phones can expose producers to interruptions twenty-four hours a day, while e-mails, accessible from a variety of devices, can be equally intrusive if mismanaged. See the exhibit "Managing E-Mail."

Managing E-Mail

E-mail messages are business records and are subject to the same compliance-type regulations as other business documents. Information contained in a producer's e-mail can provide a supporting legal record of business transactions and decisions. For this reason, agencies should develop office procedures and guidelines for producers to effectively and efficiently manage data files. Issues related to e-mail management include the following:

- E-mail creation—A producer can establish standard messages to send in response to requests for information, reducing time spent composing individual responses. Using concise language and descriptive subject lines streamlines correspondence and enhances document tracking.

- E-mail responses—Timeliness of responses is an important factor in the insurance business because coverage issues may be involved. It is important that customers receive a prompt response to inquiries and that incoming correspondence is directed to the person designated to handle specific issues. Establishing procedures to document action taken is helpful, particularly if staff may be periodically checking e-mail from an off-site location. Additionally, producers, agency principals, and agency claim representatives may want to establish automatic response systems that provide alternative contact information during nonbusiness hours.

- E-mail retention—An efficient way to handle incoming e-mail is for the producer to establish folders based on action required. For example, an "urgent" folder would contain tasks needing immediate attention, and a "delete" folder could hold messages for review and removal.

- E-mail retrieval—Producers should save and file such information as client data, correspondence, meeting notes, and coverage-related documentation. Establishing document storage guidelines streamlines the retrieval process and ensures that staff can quickly access the information needed to conduct business efficiently.

- E-mail deletion—The abundance of e-mail correspondence requires periodic review and removal of unnecessary messages. Increasing occurrences of spam (unsolicited advertising e-mail) can result in unmanageable numbers of messages.

The degree to which producers manage these issues can affect the time available to them for sales. Producers should periodically review the office procedures used to manage e-mail to ensure that customer needs are addressed and that agency information management is efficient, timely, and protective of the agency's interests.

[DA08089]

NEGOTIATION

Few skills are as valuable as the ability to negotiate. Although the term is often interpreted as getting the best possible deal from the other party, negotiations actually seek an outcome beneficial to both parties.

Negotiation is a process in which two or more parties discuss an issue and consider alternatives to reach mutual agreement. These are some basic negotiation rules and techniques:

- Know the other party
- Avoid "single-issue" negotiation

- Do not push the advantage
- Deliver more than promised

One reason people handle negotiations poorly is that they assume one side must win and the other must lose. Learning how to negotiate effectively focuses on creating the "win-win" situation. Effective negotiators consider anything other than a "win-win" to be a loss. If both sides win, both get what they want, and both are satisfied. The result is usually a positive long-term relationship that continues to benefit both parties.

Know the Other Party

Knowing the other party requires determining the other person's style of doing business and the other person's goals.

Some people are confrontational; others are nonconfrontational. Some are easygoing; others are serious. Some are talkative; others want to get straight to the point. Knowing the prospect's style of doing business helps the producer determine how to negotiate. For example, if the other party is highly competitive and wants to win at everything, one should be prepared to exert more pressure during negotiations. Likewise, dealing with an easygoing, noncompetitive party who has a relaxed way of conducting business might entail exerting less pressure.

Effective negotiation also involves understanding the other party's goals. For example, when asked the one thing every customer is seeking, one may respond, "A low price!" Although this may be true for many, it is not always the other party's top priority.

Avoid "Single-Issue" Negotiation

A "single issue" negotiation should be avoided because the result is often a "win-lose" scenario. For example, many try to avoid the price issue. However, discussing it last invites the "single issue" trap. If the parties have agreed on everything except price, one party may then spend an hour convincing the other of the value for the price.

One way to avoid the "single issue" trap is to have more issues on the table, with price being only one. For example, a producer could lay out all the major benefits the prospect wants, along with the price the producer wants. Then the producer could negotiate the items in groups. So for instance, the price can be lowered, but only if the prospect gives something back in another area—such as by accepting less coverage. Perhaps a convenient payment plan could offset a slightly higher annual premium.

Do Not Push the Advantage

Another negotiation technique involves not pushing the advantage. For example, suppose a business prospect has had difficulty obtaining insurance coverage at a reasonable price because of a series of property losses that occurred at only one of many locations the prospect owns. In the course of negotiations, the insurance producer recommends that if the prospect were to transfer business operations from the problem location to another site and sell the property that has been experiencing losses, the producer can obtain a much lower price from an insurer with that guarantee. Producers should not highlight the difficult position of such prospects. No matter how much the situation results in the producer's favor, the producer should not push the advantage. This benefits the producer, particularly if the insurance market later becomes more competitive.

Deliver More Than Promised

In quality management, the concept of delivering more than promised is expressed as "always seek to exceed customer expectations." Giving something more than promised after negotiations are complete creates an important advantage in future negotiations with the same customers. A customer may remember an unexpected bonus far more than the details of the negotiation. Such a bonus does not have to be extravagant or costly, just unexpected and pleasurable. Exceeding the customer's expectations can facilitate subsequent negotiating, and using other negotiation techniques can create lasting business relationships.

PERSONAL PRODUCTION PLAN CASE STUDY

Knowing how to apply knowledge of personal production plans, time management techniques, and negotiation strategies to the facts of a case is an important skill. By carefully considering the facts provided and answering the Knowledge to Action questions, this activity should help you make the transition from developing the skills associated with personal production plans, time management, and negotiation strategies to knowing how to apply them to a "win-win" negotiation on an account.

Case Facts

Sheila has been a producer at a property-casualty insurance agency for two years. She is eager to impress management by generating new accounts. Several small businesses, many of which are technology oriented, have recently taken root in her assigned region. Sheila believes these businesses represent an opportunity for her to increase her commercial lines sales. Because of their technological orientation, she thinks that appealing to these organizations through a combination of traditional networking (such as participating in community groups where the businesses are represented) and promoting her agency's social media marketing savvy will help her cultivate a relationship with them.

Knowledge to Action

Action Task: Review the case facts.

According to your analysis of the case facts, which one of these is the most appropriate personal mission statement for Sheila?

a. "I will use social media tools to appeal to at least one of the area's new small businesses."

b. "I will join community groups in which the area's small businesses participate."

c. "I will serve the property-casualty needs of the community."

d. "I will increase commercial lines sales."

Feedback: c. "I will serve the property-casualty needs of the community" is the most appropriate mission statement for Sheila because it is broadly stated and needs based. The other choices do not meet both of these criteria.

Case Analysis Tools

To achieve her goal, Sheila will apply her knowledge of personal production plans to devise one that describes what she will accomplish, how she will accomplish it, and when it will be accomplished. She will then use her time management and negotiation skills to fulfill the plan.

Overview of Steps

Sheila will follow these high-level steps to pursue her goals:

- Devise a personal production plan
- Use time management techniques to organize the activities needed to achieve her objectives
- Apply negotiation skills to achieve a "win-win" negotiation on an account

Devise a Personal Production Plan

In order to devise a personal production plan, Sheila follows a seven-step process:

- Develop a mission statement
- Develop goals
- Develop strategies
- Develop objectives

- Develop budgets
- Establish policies and procedures
- Monitor the plan

Sheila knows that an effective mission statement should be broadly stated and needs based, so she settles on, "I will serve the property-casualty needs of the community." Armed with this mission statement, she next develops goals based on the mission statement and her general ideas about attracting new insureds. She also realizes that her agency needs to increase its commercial lines business and wants to establish a stronger presence in the increasingly competitive regional market. Sheila is eager to prove that she can help the agency achieve these objectives and wants to negotiate a production sales goal that challenges her and satisfies the agency. She focuses on developing specific, measureable, achievable, relevant, and time-bound statements that encapsulate ways she can appeal to the local technology organizations she wants to engage during the plan year.

Knowledge to Action

Action Task: Review the case facts and Sheila's mission statement.

According to your analysis of the case facts and Sheila's mission statement, which one of these is an appropriate goal for Sheila?

a. "I will increase my commercial sales commissions this year."
b. "During calendar year 20X1, I will generate 15 percent more annualized commissions for commercial property insurance than I did during the last year."
c. "I will use traditional networking and social media tools to cultivate relationships with local small businesses."
d. "I will improve my social networking acumen."

Feedback: b. "During calendar year 20X1, I will generate 15 percent more annualized commissions for commercial property insurance than I did during the last year" is the most appropriate goal because, unlike the others, it is specific (focusing on commercial property), measureable (her previous year's commissions may be compared to the following year's), achievable (15 percent is a realistic increase), relevant (the goal stems from her mission statement and her agency's needs), and time-bound ("during calendar year 20X1").

Sheila uses her goal, "During calendar year 20X1, I will generate 15 percent more annualized commissions for commercial property insurance than I did during the last year," to develop strategies that indicate specific ways she can achieve it and, by extension, her mission. These strategies should be personal to Sheila, relate to the agency's mission and goals, and narrow the focus of her personal activities, while remaining broad enough to allow a variety of sales activities, including traditional networking and use of social media.

Knowledge to Action

Action Task: Review the case facts, Sheila's mission statement, and Sheila's goal.

According to your analysis of the case facts and her mission statement, which of these are appropriate strategies for Sheila?

a. Providing total risk control services for small businesses
b. Using social media and traditional networking to target small businesses with commercial coverage needs
c. Participating in meetings of the local chapter of the Small Business Administration
d. Developing technical expertise in the commercial insurance needs of small businesses

Feedback: a., b., and d. all strike a balance between generality and specificity while sufficiently narrowing Shelia's sales activities in the context of her personal goals and her agency's objectives. To participate in meetings of the local chapter of the Small Business Administration, though a useful endeavor, may be too specific to constitute a strategy.

Next, Sheila uses her strategies to develop objectives. See the exhibit "Sample Strategies and Objectives for Sheila, the Producer."

Sample Strategies and Objectives for Sheila, the Producer

Strategy: Providing total risk control services for small businesses

- "I will research the Web sites, promotional materials, and publicly available documents related to five of the area's technologically oriented small businesses by January 21, 20X1."

- "I will use my research to develop appropriate risk control strategies for each of the five businesses by March 31, 20X1."

- "I will present my findings to my fellow producers by May 20X1."

Strategy: Using social media and traditional networking to target small businesses with commercial coverage needs

- "I will attend at least two workshops for new small business owners held by the local chapter of the Small Business Association by June 20X1."

- "I will use social media to develop and cultivate contacts with at least ten representatives from local small businesses by May 20X1."

- "I will author a blog on the agency's Web site that focuses on leveraging social media opportunities by June 20X1."

[DA08201]

Shelia must next determine how to budget her time to execute the strategies directed at achieving her overall goal, "During calendar year 20X1, I will generate 15 percent more annualized commissions for commercial property insurance than I did during the last year." This goal focuses on effective selling. Selling requires efficient use of time. Therefore, Sheila decides to examine how she can apply time management techniques to the daily activities she will direct toward fulfilling her objectives.

Use Time Management Techniques

Sheila studies her first strategy of providing total risk control services for small businesses. To utilize this strategy, she must fulfill the objectives listed in the "Sample Strategies and Objectives for Sheila, the Producer" exhibit. Sheila refines these objectives by determining which businesses she will target and creates a "To Do" list with tasks that involve researching each organization. This entails daily Web searches, phone calls, and in-person meetings. She plans to simultaneously research risk control strategies for these firms, determine the best way to integrate social media into her sales pitch, devise topics for her blog, and find ways to participate in local organizations and "town hall" meetings in which these organizations participate. Meanwhile, she must continue to service her existing customers, many of whom have become accustomed to her hands-on approach to coverage and claim resolution.

As 20X1 begins, Sheila is intimidated by the sheer volume of work that seems to separate her from the goals in her production plan. Because she is especially skilled at dealing with her existing customers, she tends to devote a large portion of each day to their phone calls and e-mails. Though she realizes the importance of her research and in developing contacts with the businesses she wishes to target, she often finds herself delaying the related tasks to attend to more pressing matters, or simply neglecting tasks that appear too large for her to confront within the allotted time.

Knowledge to Action

Action Task: Review the elements of Sheila's production plan and the approach she's adopted to pursuing it.

Identify time-wasters that may be impeding Sheila's progress toward her goal.

Feedback: Time-wasters that may be impeding Sheila's progress toward her goal include these:

- Telephone and e-mail interruptions—Sheila's devotion to her insureds may be causing her to allow their e-mails and phone calls to disrupt her other tasks too frequently.
- Inadequate planning—Although Sheila has listed her long-term goals and assigned them specific due dates in her objectives, they may be too general to be useful.

- Attempting too much—Sheila's goals require her to balance a substantial amount of office work and field work with the tasks associated with her existing customers.
- Lack of self-discipline; procrastination—Intimidated by her workload, Sheila recognizes that she is delaying tasks that are not directly related to servicing clients or that appear too large for her to accomplish.

Sheila recognizes that many of the time-wasters that imperil accomplishment of her goals could be mitigated or eliminated by setting more specific priorities. When faced with a new task, she decides to label it according to four priority levels:

- Important and urgent (As)
- Important but not urgent (Bs)
- Urgent but not important (Cs)
- Not important and not urgent (Ds)

One day, Shelia identifies three tasks that she would like to complete:

- Work on a blog entry due for submission to the agency sales manager by the end of the following week
- Answer questions about changes to the Business Auto Coverage Form left on the agency's social networking site from two local small business owners
- Compile research on a local small business's Web site

While Sheila is considering these tasks, an existing insured sends an e-mail checking on the status of a claim he filed several days previously that is being reviewed by the insurer.

Knowledge to Action

Action Task: Review the elements of Sheila's production plan, the approach she's adopted to pursuing it, the four priority levels, and the tasks she is considering completing on this particular day.

Assign a priority level to each of the four tasks Sheila would like to accomplish.

Feedback: The priority levels Sheila would assign to these tasks are these:

- Write blog entry—This could be labeled as important but not urgent (B), because, although it is tethered directly to one of Sheila's goals, a brief blog entry due the following week should not take precedence over more pressing tasks that are more directly related to her goal.
- Answer questions on social networking site—Because this entails impressing potential insureds with social networking acumen and insurance expertise, it should be considered important and urgent (A).

- Compile research on Web site—This task, which directly relates to accomplishment of an objective that is directly related to her goal of increasing her commercial lines commissions, could be considered important and urgent (A) as well.

- Respond to insured's e-mail—This could be labeled as important but not urgent (B), because the insured's claim is being addressed by the insurer and Sheila has recently been in contact with this insured. She should reply to the message in the time she has allotted to respond to other e-mails as part of her overall time management strategy.

Apply Negotiation Skills

One of the small technology businesses with whom Sheila has interacted on her agency's social networking Web site eventually agrees to meet with her to discuss some of the risk control services her agency could offer. She hopes that the meeting will be the beginning of a relationship that will eventually allow her to acquire their business.

When negotiating an actual deal with this prospect, Sheila would like to strike a "win-win" resolution that delivers appropriate insurance coverage and risk control services to the insured while also helping her achieve her goal of increased commercial lines commissions. Because she has thoroughly researched the company, she believes she will be able to speak intelligently about its risk control goals. Knowing the other party is a key component of effective negotiation.

Sheila's research reveals that this company's technology-based systems can be damaged and its security unintentionally or intentionally compromised by the organization's employees or by customers and suppliers. She concludes that the use of such systems increases the organization's exposure to property, net income, and liability loss and develops a risk control and mitigation strategy that focuses on cyber risk and appropriate coverage. Indeed, this business has emphasized its concern about these issues in the correspondence it has had with Sheila since its initial connection on the agency's social networking site. Because she is focused on her goal, "During calendar year 20X1, I will generate 15 percent more annualized commissions for commercial property insurance than I did during the last year," she decides that she will first negotiate with the company to determine the price with which it is comfortable before discussing coverage specifics.

Knowledge to Action

Action Task: Review the elements of Sheila's production plan, the information she has developed about this sales prospect, and her planned approach to the negotiation.

If Sheila focuses only on price initially, identify the negotiating trap into which she could potentially fall.

Feedback: If Sheila focuses only on price, she risks causing the negotiation to focus on a single issue. Producers should try to avoid "single issue" negotiation because the result is often a "win-lose" scenario.

Among the specifications included in the agency's sales management policies and procedures are provisions that entail the agency sales manager meeting with Sheila (as well as other producers on staff) weekly to monitor her plan, review her progress toward her goals, and to coach her along the way, as needed.

SUMMARY

A personal production plan consists of the producer's mission statement, goals, strategies, objectives, budgets, policies, and procedures. It is developed using seven steps:

1. Develop a mission statement.
2. Develop goals.
3. Develop strategies.
4. Develop objectives.
5. Determine budgets.
6. Establish policies and procedures.
7. Monitor the plan.

Agency managers ask each producer to complete a personal producer production plan. They combine these individual production plans into summaries, which typically form the basis for the agency's annual sales plan.

After developing a personal production plan, a producer must find the time to sell. Producers can use these five strategies to manage time effectively:

- Eliminate time-wasters
- Set priorities
- Prepare for meetings
- Plan
- Manage phone calls and e-mails

R. Alec Mackenzie, a time management expert, cites twenty major time-wasters that should be identified and reduced or eliminated. In a time management system, a producer allocates business time by assigning priorities to business activities.

Important negotiating rules and techniques include these:

- Know the other party
- Avoid "single-issue" negotiation
- Do not push the advantage
- Deliver more than promised

Knowing how to apply knowledge of personal production plans, time management techniques, and negotiation strategies is crucial to a producer's ability to fulfill his or her personal production goals.

ASSIGNMENT NOTES

1. R. Alec Mackenzie, The Time Trap (New York: AMACOM, American Management Association, 1997), p. 61.
2. Stephen R. Covey, The 7 Habits of Highly Effective People (New York: Simon & Schuster, 1990), p. 165.

AAI 83A Course Guide

Contents

 ## Study Materials Available for AAI 83A

Agency Operations and Sales Management—Principles of Agency Management, 4th ed., 2011, AICPCU.

AAI 83 Segment A SMART Study Aids—Review Notes and Flash Cards, 1st ed.

▶▶

Student Resources

Catalog A complete listing of our offerings can be found in The Institutes' professional development catalog, including information about:

- Current programs and courses
- Current textbooks, course guides, SMART Study Aids, and online offerings
- Program completion requirements

To obtain a copy of the catalog, visit our website at www.TheInstitutes.org or contact Customer Service at (800) 644-2101.

How to Prepare for Institutes Exams This free handbook is designed to help you by:

- Giving you ideas on how to use textbooks and course guides as effective learning tools
- Providing steps for answering exam questions effectively
- Recommending exam-day strategies

The handbook is printable from the Student Services Center on The Institutes' website at www.TheInstitutes.org, or available by calling Customer Service at (800) 644-2101.

Educational Counseling Services To ensure that you take courses matching both your needs and your skills, you can obtain free counseling from The Institutes by:

- Emailing your questions to Advising@TheInstitutes.org
- Calling an Institutes' counselor directly at (610) 644-2100, ext. 7601
- Obtaining and completing a self-inventory form, available on our website at www.TheInstitutes.org or by contacting Customer Service at (800) 644-2101

Exam Registration Information As you proceed with your studies, be sure to arrange for your exam.

- If you are taking this course through a class, check with your instructor for information on how to register for the exam.
- Plan to register in advance of your exam.

How to Contact The Institutes For more information on any of these publications and services:

- Visit our website at www.TheInstitutes.org
- Call us at (800) 644-2101 or (610) 644-2100 outside the U.S.
- Email us at CustomerService@TheInstitutes.org
- Fax us at (610) 640-9576
- Write to us at The Institutes, Customer Service, 720 Providence Road, Suite 100, Malvern, PA 19355-3433

Using This Course Guide

This course guide will help you learn the course content and prepare for the exam.

Each assignment in this course guide typically includes the following components:

Educational Objectives These are the most important study tools in the course guide. Because all of the questions on the exam are based on the Educational Objectives, the best way to study for the exam is to focus on these objectives.

Each Educational Objective typically begins with one of the following action words, which indicate the level of understanding required for the exam:

Analyze—Determine the nature and the relationship of the parts.

Apply—Put to use for a practical purpose.

Associate—Bring together into relationship.

Calculate—Determine numeric values by mathematical process.

Classify—Arrange or organize according to class or category.

Compare—Show similarities and differences.

Contrast—Show only differences.

Define—Give a clear, concise meaning.

Describe—Represent or give an account.

Determine—Settle or decide.

Evaluate—Determine the value or merit.

Explain—Relate the importance or application.

Identify or list—Name or make a list.

Illustrate—Give an example.

Justify—Show to be right or reasonable.

Paraphrase—Restate in your own words.

Recommend—Suggest or endorse something to be used.

Summarize—Concisely state the main points.

Outline The outline lists the topics in the assignment. Read the outline before the required reading to become familiar with the assignment content and the relationships of topics.

Key Words and Phrases These words and phrases are fundamental to understanding the assignment and have a common meaning for those working in insurance. After completing the required reading, test your understanding of the assignment's Key Words and Phrases by writing their definitions.

Review Questions The review questions test your understanding of what you have read. Review the Educational Objectives and required reading, then answer the questions to the best of your ability. When you are finished, check the answers at the end of the assignment to evaluate your comprehension.

Application Questions These questions continue to test your knowledge of the required reading by applying what you've studied to "hypothetical" real-life situations. Again, check the suggested answers at the end of the assignment to review your progress.

Sample Exam On the inside of the cover, your course guide includes a code for accessing SMART Online Practice Exams. Use the option available for the course you're taking to become familiar with the test format. SMART Online Practice Exams are as close as you can get to experiencing an actual exam before taking one.

More Study Aids

The Institutes also produce supplemental study tools, called SMART Study Aids, for many of our courses. When SMART Study Aids are available for a course, they are listed on page iii of the course guide. SMART Study Aids include Review Notes and Flash Cards and are excellent tools to help you learn and retain the information in each assignment.

1

Agency Formation and Environment

Educational Objectives

After learning the content of this assignment, you should be able to:

1. Describe the principal-agent relationship in terms of the following:
   - Duties an agent owes to the principal
   - Remedies a principal has for an agent's breach of duties
   - Duties a principal owes to an agent
   - Remedies an agent has for a principal's breach of duties

2. Describe the insurance agency-principal relationship in terms of the following:
   - The specific duties owed by insurance agents
   - The difference between insurance agents and brokers
   - The authority of insurance agents

3. Describe producer licensing requirements.

4. Describe the major sections of an insurance agency contract, including any supplemental agreements.

5. Describe the following forms of legal ownership of an insurance agency and the advantages and/or disadvantages of each:
   - Sole proprietorships
   - Partnerships
   - Corporations.

6. Describe insurance agency operating affiliations in terms of the following:
   - The various types of operating affiliations and how they can be formed
   - The advantages and disadvantages of independent agency networks
   - How to evaluate independent agency networks

1

- How to evaluate other support organizations that an agency might affiliate with

7. Describe the purpose of each of the federal and state regulations governing insurance.

Outline

▶ **Agent's Duties and Remedies**
  A. Agent's Duties to Principal
     1. Loyalty
     2. Obedience
     3. Reasonable Care
     4. Accounting
     5. Information
  B. Principal's Remedies
  C. Principal's Duties to Agent
     1. Agreed-On Period of Employment
     2. Compensation
     3. Reimbursement for Expenses
     4. Indemnity for Losses
  D. Agent's Remedies
▶ **Insurance Producers and Agency Law**
  A. Duties of Insurance Agents
  B. Agents and Brokers Compared
  C. Authority of Insurance Agents
     1. Express Authority
     2. Implied Authority
     3. Apparent Authority
     4. Agency by Ratification
     5. Agent as Independent Contractor
     6. Agent Acting for an Undisclosed Principal
     7. Agent and a Nonexistent Principal
▶ **Producer Licensing**
  A. Producers
  B. Claim Representatives
  C. Insurance Consultants
▶ **Insurance Agency Contracts**
  A. Major Sections of an Agency Contract
     1. Term of Agreement/Termination
     2. Rehabilitation
     3. Ownership of Expirations
     4. Payment Procedures
     5. Indemnification
     6. Contract Amendments
     7. Miscellaneous Provisions

  B. Commissions
  C. Contingent Commission Agreements
▶ **Legal Forms of Organization**
  A. Sole Proprietorships
  B. Partnerships
  C. Corporations
  D. Choice of Legal Form
▶ **Operating Affiliations**
  A. Independent Agency Networks
     1. Advantages of Networks
     2. Disadvantages of Networks
     3. Evaluating Independent Agency Networks
  B. Insurance Company Affiliations
  C. Specialty Marketing Groups
  D. General Purpose Groups
  E. Common Identity Groups
  F. Evaluating Other Affiliations
     1. Services Provided
     2. Personnel
     3. Exclusivity
     4. Fees
     5. Contract
     6. Financial Strength
▶ **Insurance Producers and Regulation**
  A. Federal Regulations Affecting Insurance Producers
     1. Dodd-Frank Wall Street Reform and Consumer Protection Act
     2. Securities and Exchange Commission (SEC)
     3. Federal Emergency Management Agency (FEMA)
     4. Department of Transportation (DOT)
     5. Fair Credit Reporting Act
     6. Gramm-Leach-Bliley Act
     7. Electronic Signatures in Global and National Commerce Act (ESIGN)
     8. USA Patriot Act
     9. Sarbanes-Oxley Act
     10. CAN-SPAM Act

s.m.a.r.t. tips Don't spend time on material you have already mastered. The SMART Review Notes are organized by the Educational Objectives found in each assignment to help you track your study.

Outline

11. Telemarketing and Consumer Fraud and Abuse Prevention Act and the Do Not Call Implementation Act

B. State Regulations Affecting Insurance Producers

1. Licensing Laws
2. Unfair Trade Practices Act
3. Unfair Claims Settlement Practices Acts
4. Handling Premiums
5. Dealing With Suitable Insurers

For each assignment, you should define or describe each of the Key Words and Phrases and answer each of the Review and Application Questions.

Educational Objective 1
Describe the principal-agent relationship in terms of the following:

- **Duties an agent owes to the principal**
- **Remedies a principal has for an agent's breach of duties**
- **Duties a principal owes to an agent**
- **Remedies an agent has for a principal's breach of duties**

Key Words and Phrases

Ministerial duties

Cause of action

Review Questions

1-1. List the duties an agent owes to a principal.

1-2. List three exceptions to the rule that an agent cannot delegate to another the authority granted by a principal.

1-3. List the duties a principal owes to an agent.

1-4. Describe the agent's remedies for a principal's breach of duties.

Educational Objective 2

Describe the insurance agency-principal relationship in terms of the following:

- **The specific duties owed by insurance agents**
- **The difference between insurance agents and brokers**
- **The authority of insurance agents**

Key Words and Phrases

Dual agency

Express authority

Implied authority

Apparent authority

Ratification

Review Questions

2-1. Describe when the producer is usually representing the insurer and when the producer is usually representing the insured.

2-2. Describe when a producer is an agent or a broker.

2-3. Explain how the premium is affected when a producer charges a fee instead of receiving a commission.

2-4. Distinguish between a general agent and a special agent in terms of apparent authority.

2-5. Explain why apparent authority is often called authority by estoppel.

2-6. Describe the advantage to a principal dealing with an independent contractor instead of an employee.

Application Questions

2-7. Mary paid the premium for her personal auto policy to her insurance agent. However, her agent, Paul, did not forward her premium payment to the insurer. Instead he used the money to pay off one of his personal gambling debts. This occurred in a state that has a statute stipulating that insurance agents are agents of the insurer and not of the insured. The insurer did not receive Mary's premium and it did not issue a personal auto policy for her. When she has an accident that otherwise would have been covered had the policy been issued, what will the insurer do?

2-8. Fred and Larry are partners in an insurance brokerage firm and are weighing the advantages and disadvantages of charging fees instead of commissions for their services. They are facing a highly competitive market in which premiums are shrinking.

    a.   Fred favors charging fees for their services. What advantages of a fee system might he point out?

    b.   Larry favors charging commissions for their services. What disadvantage to a fee system might he point out?

2-9. Wiley has a claim that would have been covered under a homeowner's policy. He is arguing that his insurance agent, Charlie, had the apparent authority of an insurer when Charlie offered five years of free coverage on Wiley's luxury home as part of a special promotion. Is Wiley's argument valid? Explain your answer.

Educational Objective 3
Describe producer licensing requirements.

Review Questions

3-1. Describe regulators' ultimate goal for insurance producer licensing.

3-2. Describe some of the key benefits of the Producer Database (PDB).

3-3. Explain why it is important that the licensing of claim representatives in most states includes an examination.

Application Question

3-4. Thomas has approached Mary to be her public adjuster and insurance consultant. Mary has operations in several states and asks if she were to hire Thomas, would he need to be licensed as a public adjuster or an insurance consultant in any of those states?

    a. If Thomas responds that public adjusters are never required to be licensed, is he correct? Explain your answer.

    b. Is Thomas correct if he responds that public adjusters and insurance consultants are sometimes required to be licensed, but that because he is licensed as an insurance consultant for life-health insurance, he will never need to take a separate examination for property-casualty insurance? Explain your answer.

Educational Objective 4

Describe the major sections of an insurance agency contract, including any supplemental agreements.

Key Words and Phrases

Run-off provision

Agency bill

Direct bill

Arbitration clause

Contingent commission agreement

Review Questions

4-1. What are the major sections of an insurance agency contract?

4-2. Many insurance agency contracts set an indefinite term of agreement/termina-
      tion by allowing the insurer to terminate the contract for any reason as long as
      the specified notice is given. Explain how this approach may put the agent at a
      disadvantage.

4-3. An insurance agency's ownership of its book of business is well established
      by court cases, but explain how the specific wording in an insurance agency
      contract often varies.

4-4. Describe several of the questions an insurance agency contract should clearly answer when addressing billing issues.

4-5. Why is the arbitration clause an important part of an insurance agency contract?

4-6. Describe what a contingent commission agreement is.

Application Question

4-7. Atwell Insurance Company has just provided Jamal Wilson, an independent insurance agent and agency principal of the Wilson Agency, with the agency contract for his review. For each of the seven sections Jamal is likely to find in the contract, describe some of the issues Jamal should negotiate to develop a favorable agency arrangement with Atwell Insurance.

Educational Objective 5

Describe the following forms of legal ownership of an insurance agency and the advantages and/or disadvantages of each:

- **Sole proprietorships**
- **Partnerships**
- **Corporations.**

Key Words and Phrases

Sole proprietorship

Partnership

Corporation

S corporation

Limited liability company (LLC)

Review Questions

5-1. Describe the different legal forms of organization an agency may choose.

5-2. Describe the only requirements that must be met for operating an insurance agency as a sole proprietorship.

5-3. In a partnership, every partner has a fiduciary relationship with the other partners and with the business. Describe what fiduciary duties impose on the partners.

5-4. Describe two types of partnerships that are available.

5-5. How do most closely held corporations dispose of the stock of a departing stockholder?

Application Question

5-6. Paul is starting his own insurance agency. He is considering the advantages and disadvantages of the different legal forms of organization for his agency.

   a. Paul is not comfortable with personal liability and would prefer to shield his personal assets. Which legal forms limit the liability of an agency's owners?

   b. Paul is concerned that if he becomes disabled or dies the agency will not survive, leaving his employees unemployed and his customers without an agency to service their needs. Which legal forms create an agency with a life of its own that will continue despite the poor health of its owner?

   c. If Paul wants to use one of the three types of corporate forms but would prefer to have the earnings of his agency taxed only once and not separately from his own personal income, which legal forms should he consider?

Educational Objective 6

Describe insurance agency operating affiliations in terms of the following:

- **The various types of operating affiliations and how they can be formed**
- **The advantages and disadvantages of independent agency networks**
- **How to evaluate independent agency networks**
- **How to evaluate other support organizations that an agency might affiliate with**

Key Word or Phrase

Independent agency network

Review Questions

6-1. What are independent agency groups also known as?

6-2. As agencies determine whether to join independent agency networks, they perform what five activities?

6-3.   For what purpose do insurers form networks of affiliated agencies?

6-4.   How are the costs of operating general purpose groups and common identity groups paid?

6-5.   Understanding that the individuals behind the service provided by a support organization ultimately determine the success of any affiliation, how does a producer considering affiliation evaluate a support organization's personnel?

Application Question

6-6.   Gilbert is the owner of an insurance agency. He has worked several decades building up his business. He is now considering affiliating with various other agencies and support organizations. However, he has several concerns.

a.   Gilbert is concerned he will not retain ownership of his clients' policy expirations if he joins in a network with other agencies. How might the owner of another agency that wants to affiliate with Gilbert's agency respond to this concern?

b. Gilbert is being asked to draft a questionnaire of what he and other agency owners want to know about each other's agencies. What information should he consider asking?

c. After reviewing the results from his questionnaire, Gilbert is concerned about the needed start-up capital, the projected cash flow, and the costs of the new network. What can Gilbert do with his fellow agency owners to address these concerns?

d. Gilbert would like to learn how other successful producers from other areas of the country address similar problems and concerns. What group can he affiliate with that may provide an opportunity to meet with such producers and discuss these types of issues?

Educational Objective 7
Describe the purpose of each of the federal and state regulations governing insurance.

Key Words and Phrases

Countersignature laws

Unfair trade practices

Review Questions

7-1. Explain why the Securities and Exchange Commission regulates variable life insurance but not property-casualty insurance.

7-2. Explain what rights an insurance applicant has when an insurer acts based on information contained in an applicant's consumer report.

7-3. What is the purpose of the Sarbanes-Oxley Act?

7-4. Describe what countersignature laws require.

7-5. Describe what individuals engaging in unfair trade practices may be subject to.

Application Questions

7-6. William operates an insurance agency. He earns a high percentage of his commission income from other agents who must comply with countersignature laws and share their commissions with him for serving as a resident producer for their insureds. William's daughter Sally wants to take over the agency from her dad. What should William warn Sally about regarding the continuation of commission income from other agents complying with countersignature laws?

7-7. Mike and Phil co-own an insurance agency. Phil often collects premiums from insureds on an insurer's behalf and commingles the money in his personal account. He earns a higher interest rate by maintaining a higher balance in his account. He carefully keeps track of what amounts belong to him and what amounts need to be forwarded to an insurer. No one is accusing Phil of stealing, but Mike is concerned. Is Mike's concern warranted? Explain your answer.

Answers to Assignment 1 Questions

NOTE: These answers are provided to give students a basic understanding of acceptable types of responses. They often are not the only valid answers and are not intended to provide an exhaustive response to the questions.

Educational Objective 1

1-1. An agent's implied duties to a principal include these:

- Loyalty

- Obedience

- Reasonable care

- Accounting

- Information

1-2. These three exceptions apply to the nondelegation rule:

- Ministerial duties—If certain tasks do not require judgment or discretion, an agent can delegate their performance.

- Customary appointments—If custom and usage of a particular business involve the delegation of authority, the agent can delegate.

- Emergency appointments—In an emergency that requires the appointment of another to protect the principal's interests, the agent can make an emergency appointment.

1-3. The principal owes these duties to the agent:

- Agreed-on period of employment

- Compensation

- Reimbursement for expenses

- Indemnity for losses

1-4. An agent can sue for compensation, indemnity, or reimbursement and can also obtain a court order requiring an accounting from the principal. An agent discharged by a principal during a specified employment period can sue for compensation for the remainder of the period. An agent can also exercise a lien, or right to retain possession of the principal's goods, until the principal has paid the amounts due.

Educational Objective 2

2-1. The producer usually represents the insurer when binding insurance, keeping records, collecting premiums, and issuing and canceling policies. The producer usually represents the customer when suggesting and selecting coverages or insurers.

2-2. Whether an insurance producer is an agent or a broker depends on whose interests the producer represents. When representing the insurance buyer, the producer is a broker. When representing the insurance seller (an insurer), the producer is an agent.

2-3. When a broker charges a fee, the insurance is usually "written net" by the insurer; that is, the premium is reduced to eliminate the producer commission.

2-4. A general agent has authority to perform all acts that are usual and customary in such a capacity. For example, a construction project general manager or a stockbroker managing an investment portfolio conducts a series of transactions for a principal on an ongoing basis.

A special agent is usually restricted to performing just those acts essential to the situation. A special agent may conduct a single transaction or a small group of transactions for the principal on a limited-term basis, such as a stockbroker asked to purchase a certain number of shares in a specific company.

2-5. Apparent authority is often called authority by estoppel on the theory that if a principal creates the appearance of authority in an agent and a third party reasonably relies on that appearance, the principal should be estopped (prevented) from denying that authority.

2-6. A principal dealing with an independent contractor has the advantage of avoiding liability for the actions of the independent contractor; whereas an employer is responsible for an employee's actions that are performed within the scope of the employment.

2-7. The insurer will cover the accident as if it had received Mary's premium. Since Mary paid Paul in a state that has a statute stipulating an insurance agent is an agent of the insurer, payment made to the agent is binding on the insurer.

2-8. These answers address Fred and Larry's decision of whether to charge fees or commissions for their services:

a. The potential for conflicts of interest is minimized because the insurer does not pay a commission. Additionally, the fee can reflect the amount of compensation the broker requires for service, overhead, and profit. In a competitive market in which premiums (and therefore commissions) are shrinking, the broker's fee may remain constant or even increase.

b. Fees are visible to the insurance buyer, whereas the commission is part of the premium. Knowing the fees that are charged, an insured can evaluate the cost of producer service separately from the cost of insurance protection and can negotiate the fee separately.

2-9. The concept of apparent authority may appear to be unfair to an insurer, the principal, but its result is to protect innocent insureds, allowing them to recover from the principal when the principal has made it appear, either intentionally or unintentionally, that the agent has authority to act.

Wiley, however, cannot depend so completely on appearances created by Charlie, his agent. The public, which includes Wiley, has a responsibility to protect itself and must always be alert to unusual situations. When Charlie acted in a way that appeared to be adverse to the best interests of the insurer (by giving away five years of coverage on a luxury home for free), Wiley had a duty to determine the extent of Charlie's authority by a direct inquiry to the insurer.

Educational Objective 3

3-1. Regulators' ultimate goal is to move beyond reciprocity and to resolve issues related to uniformity in producer licensing. Meeting this goal will streamline the licensing process while retaining state regulatory authority over it.

3-2. Some of the key benefits of the PDB are increased productivity, lower cost, reduction of paper, access to real-time information, and the ability to conduct national verification of the license and status of a producer.

3-3. Licensing of claim representatives in most states includes an examination, which is important because of the complex and technical nature of insurance policies and the claim process.

3-4. These answers deal with Mary's hiring Thomas as an insurance consultant and public adjuster:

   a. Thomas should know that public adjusters, who represent insureds for a fee, are generally required to be licensed to ensure technical competence and to protect the public, which includes Mary.

   b. Thomas should know that separate examinations are usually required to be an insurance consultant in both life-health insurance and property-casualty insurance.

Educational Objective 4

4-1. These are the seven major provisions of agency contracts:

   • The term of agreement/termination

   • Rehabilitation

   • Ownership of expirations

   • Payment procedures

   • Indemnification

   • Contract amendments

   • Miscellaneous provisions

4-2. This approach may put the agent at a disadvantage by making it difficult to perform long-term planning with any assurance that the insurer will continue the relationship.

4-3. Some insurers require joint ownership of expirations. Some contracts allow insurers to claim ownership from the agency if the contract is terminated for certain reasons. Other contracts require the agency to give the insurer a security interest in the expirations.

4-4. An insurance agency contract should address billing issues by clearly answering several questions such as these:

   • Which types of business will be put on direct bill and which on agency bill?

   • For agency bill, when will the premiums be due for new business, renewals, and changes or endorsements?

   • Will the agency collect the first premium payment on a direct billed policy?

   • How prominently will the agency name be displayed on direct bill communications with an insured?

4-5. The arbitration clause provides a formal method for the agency and insurer to resolve disagreements arising under the agency contract. The parties should first make good faith efforts to settle any disagreements, but, if they fail, an arbitration agreement is often a cost-effective alternative to litigation or contract termination.

4-6. A contingent commission agreement is a contract provision in which an insurer agrees to make supplemental payments to producers based on profitability alone or on a combination of profitability, volume, and growth in the agency's book of business placed with that insurer.

4-7. Answers will vary. However, you should be able to justify your answers based on concepts presented and on any agency contracts you may have encountered. Following are examples of some of the issues Jamal should negotiate within the contract provisions to develop a favorable agency arrangement with Atwell.

   a. Within the term of agreement/termination provision, Jamal may negotiate how and when Atwell can cancel the agency contract. He should negotiate for a specific contract term, with automatic renewal or rollover unless he violates the contract. This provision helps Jamal engage in long-term agency planning. Additionally, Jamal should negotiate that that the contract not allow for agency termination based on volume alone or mix of business business alone unless this has been previously agreed upon in writing. Jamal should also consider negotiating the run-off provision, perhaps seeking at least a twelve month renewal cycle per policy expiration from the date of insurer notice of contract termination. This cycle will give Jamal and his staff time to replace coverage elsewhere for his customers, should he wish to retain their business.

   b. Within the terms of the rehabilitation provision, one issue that Jamal might consider negotiating is the rehabilitation period. This period should be a minimum of one year to enable Jamal and his staff to avoid agency termination.

   c. Within the terms of the ownership of expirations provision, one issue that Jamal could negotiate relates to who controls the customer relationship. This is typically determined based on whether he agency contract is an exclusive agency contract under which the insurer owns the expirations and therefore owns the customer relationship, or an independent agency or brokerage contract, under which the agency principal owns the agency and controls the customer relationship. Jamal, as the agency principal and independent insurance agent, should seek to own the policy expirations and control its customer relationships.

   d. Within the terms of the payment procedures provision, Jamal can negotiate the terms for premium billing responsibilities, whether those billings will be direct bill, agency bill, or a combination of both, and remittance procedures. An additional issue Jamal could negotiate is whether Atwell will accept full responsibility for all errors and omissions arising from direct bill procedures.

   e. Within the terms of the indemnification provision, Jamal should take care that the contract does not base its indemnification of the agency on a contributory negligence standard. Additionally, Jamal should seek to require that the insurer provide him with legal defense in an E&O claim.

f. Within the terms of the contract amendments provision, Jamal should consider the issue that although he and Atwell can agree to amend the agency contract at any time. Atwell may be free to make unilateral changes. Jamal should seek a 180-day minimum on the period during which the insurer can make unilateral changes, allowing Jamal adequate time for agency planning. Additionally, Jamal should negotiate agreements that any contract amendments will be strictly by mutual agreement and, to help the agency balance its financial planning, that any changes to commission schedules be maintained for at least twelve months.

g. Within the terms of the miscellaneous provisions, which typically include provisions relating to arbitration and the sale of the agency, Jamal may want to ensure that the arbitration clause requires Atwell to make good faith efforts to settle any disagreements, for example, a commission disagreement, before resorting to arbitration. Regarding the sale of the agency, because Jamal is an independent agent, he typically is free to sell the agency to whomever he wishes. However, the agency contract should specify terms for notifying the insurer of such a sale and for transferring the customer policies to the new owner's agency.

Educational Objective 5

5-1. An agency may choose one of the following legal forms of organization:

- Sole proprietorship—a business owned by a single individual who assumes all personal and tax liability for the business

- Partnership—a voluntary association of two or more persons who are co-owners and who agree to share in its profits and losses

- Corporation—an independent legal entity owned by stockholders and managed by a board of directors elected by the stockholders

5-2. The only requirements that must be met for operating an insurance agency as a sole proprietorship are obtaining a license issued by the state insurance regulatory authority and, in most jurisdictions, making a filing in compliance with fictitious trade name regulations if the sole proprietor's name is not the name under which the agency is to be operated.

5-3. Fiduciary duties impose a high degree of mutual trust, loyalty, and good faith on the partners just as they do on agents or trustees.

5-4. A partnership can be either a general partnership or a limited partnership. In a general partnership, all the owners are general partners with all the rights and obligations of a partner who operates the enterprise. A limited partnership includes at least one general partner and at least one limited partner, although there can be many partners in either category.

5-5. Most closely held corporations (those owned by only a few stockholders) have a written buy and sell agreement giving surviving stockholders the right and obligation to acquire the stock of a departing stockholder.

5-6. These answers address Paul's selection of a legal form of organization for his agency:

a. Paul should not use a sole proprietorship or a general partnership, which has unlimited personal liability for debts to its owners. A limited partnership, a corporation, an S corporation, or a limited liability company can provide him liability protection.

b.   Corporations, S corporations, and limited liability companies have a life beyond their owners. The ownership of one of these three types of organization is through shares of stock that can be given away, sold, or willed.

c.   Paul should consider using an S corporation or limited liability company type of corporation to avoid having corporate earnings taxed separately.

Educational Objective 6

6-1. Independent agent networks are also known as agent groups, agent clusters, or agent alliances.

6-2. Five activities are performed as agencies determine whether to join independent agency networks:

a.   Develop a questionnaire

b.   Inventory insurers

c.   Decide whether to move

d.   Appoint start-up committees

e.   Decide on a structure for the board of directors

6-3. Insurers form networks of affiliated agencies for the purpose of marketing specialized products, such as group commercial or personal insurance.

6-4. The costs of operating general purpose groups and common identity groups are paid by the annual fees of each affiliated agency or participating firm.

6-5. A producer who is considering affiliation must check references given by those in the support organization to be certain not only that the people are reliable but also that they are experienced insurance professionals.

6-6. These answers deal with Gilbert's concerns:

a.   What Gilbert is concerned about occurs in a merger, not in an independent agency network. Retaining ownership of policy expirations is an area that distinguishes a network affiliation from a merger.

b.   Gilbert should focus the questionnaire on information such as business mix, premium income, numbers of accounts, commission income, percentage of direct-billed business, information technology (IT) capabilities, staffing, plans for perpetuation, areas of specialization and expertise, agency goals, loss ratios, areas of interest to the agency principals, and level of commitment toward beginning a network.

c.   Gilbert and his fellow owners can appoint a financial start-up committee to address these concerns.

d.   General purpose groups provide this service for producers to meet one another from different areas of the country to discuss common issues.

Educational Objective 7

7-1. The Supreme Court has ruled, for regulatory purposes, that variable life insurance is a security rather than an insurance policy. To sell this product legally, a producer must hold a federal securities license and abide by federal regulations. Property-casualty insurance does not have any investment features that would subject it to federal securities laws.

7-2. When an insurer acts based on information contained in an applicant's report, the applicant has the right to ask the insurer which company provided the information. The consumer reporting company must then inform the applicant of its findings. The applicant can challenge the information. The applicant's version of the information must be added to the file by the reporting company and given to those who inquire about that individual.

7-3. The purpose of the Sarbanes-Oxley Act of 2002 is to introduce reforms to enhance corporate responsibility, enhance financial disclosures, and combat corporate and accounting fraud.

7-4. Countersignature laws require all policies covering subjects of insurance within a state to be signed by a resident producer licensed in that state.

7-5. Individuals engaging in unfair trade practices may be subject to cease and desist orders, loss of licenses, or heavy fines.

7-6. William should warn Sally that countersignature laws are facing strong challenges and are being eliminated because some regulators believe they are archaic and unnecessary, and because some courts believe they place unconstitutional restrictions on interstate commerce. Consequently, the agency may soon lose the commission income from other agents.

7-7. Yes, Mike should be concerned. Premium handling regulations directly affect producers. A producer, such as Phil, collects insurance premiums on an insurer's behalf and acts as the insurer's fiduciary for these premiums. In many states, the premiums must be kept in a separate trust account and must not be commingled with other personal or business funds. Failure to comply with this requirement can subject producers to civil and criminal penalties, including fines, loss of license, and imprisonment.

Direct Your Learning

Organizational Management

Educational Objectives

After learning the content of this assignment, you should be able to:

1. Describe the four major functions of management including these specific aspects of planning:

    - Characteristics of a plan

    - Types of plans

    - Steps in the planning process

2. Describe these specific aspects of the organizing function of management:

    - Determining forms of organizational structure

    - Developing organizational position descriptions

    - Evaluating staffing needs

3. Explain how managers lead employees by motivating, delegating, and managing conflict.

4. Describe these specific aspects of the controlling function of management:

    - The four steps in the control process

    - The factors managers should consider when evaluating employee performance

Outline

▶ **Organizational Management and Planning**
- A. Planning
  - 1. Plan Characteristics
  - 2. Plan Types
- B. Planning Process
  - 1. Develop a Mission Statement
  - 2. Develop Goals
  - 3. Develop Strategies
  - 4. Develop Objectives
  - 5. Develop Budgets
  - 6. Establish Policies and Procedures
  - 7. Monitor the Plan

▶ **Organizational Management and Organizing**
- A. Structure
  - 1. Line Organization
  - 2. Functional Organization
  - 3. Line and Staff Organization
- B. Position Descriptions
- C. Position Qualifications
- D. Evaluating Staffing Needs
  - 1. Completing Staffing Projections
  - 2. Prospecting for Employees
  - 3. Evaluating Candidates

▶ **Organizational Management and Leading**
- A. Motivating
  - 1. Money
  - 2. Security
  - 3. Recognition
  - 4. Work Importance and Responsibility
  - 5. Status
  - 6. Advancement
  - 7. Goals
  - 8. Incentives
- B. Delegating
- C. Managing Conflict
  - 1. Emphasize Superordinate Goals
  - 2. Focus on the Problem, Not the People
  - 3. Focus on Interests, Not Demands
  - 4. Create New Options for Joint Gain
  - 5. Focus on What Is Fair

▶ **Organizational Management and Controlling**
- A. Control Process
  - 1. Establishing Performance Standards
  - 2. Measuring Results
  - 3. Comparing Results With Chosen Performance Standards
  - 4. Evaluating Results and Implementing Corrective Action
- B. Employee Performance Evaluation

s.m.a.r.t. tips

Actively capture information by using the open space in the SMART Review Notes to write out key concepts. Putting information into your own words is an effective way to push that information into your memory.

For each assignment, you should define or describe each of the Key Words and Phrases and answer each of the Review and Application Questions.

Educational Objective 1

Describe the four major functions of management including these specific aspects of planning:

- **Characteristics of a plan**
- **Types of plans**
- **Steps in the planning process**

Key Words and Phrases

Management

Corporate plan

Business plan (divisional plan)

Functional plan

Management by exception

Review Questions

1-1. List the four functions of management.

1-2. Describe the four characteristics of an effective organizational plan.

1-3. Describe the characteristics of corporate organizational plans.

1-4. Contrast a mission statement with a vision statement.

1-5. Explain why budgets are an integral part of the planning process.

1-6. Describe the capital budgeting process.

1-7. Contrast policies with procedures.

Educational Objective 2

Describe these specific aspects of the organizing function of management:

- **Determining forms of organizational structure**
- **Developing organizational position descriptions**
- **Evaluating staffing needs**

Key Words and Phrases

Line organization

Functional organization

Line and staff organization

Review Questions

2-1. Explain how a line organizational structure operates.

2-2. Describe the advantages of a line organizational structure.

2-3. Describe the greatest disadvantage of a line organization.

2-4. Describe the advantage of a functional organizational structure.

2-5. Describe the disadvantages of a line and staff organizational structure.

2-6. Identify the areas included in a position description.

2-7. Explain why adequate staffing is important to an organization.

2-8. Describe the benefits of prospecting for employees in anticipation of future organizational needs.

2-9. Describe the methods an organization can use to prospect for additional employees.

2-10. Identify the tasks in the candidate evaluation process.

2-11. Explain how employers can make a formal employment offer once the hiring decision is made.

Educational Objective 3
Explain how managers lead employees by motivating, delegating, and managing conflict.

Key Words and Phrases

Integrative bargaining

Distributive negotiation

Review Questions

3-1. List the three major aspects of leadership that are most important for insurance agency management.

3-2. Explain why needs are an important element in motivating employees.

3-3. Explain how money can be a negative motivation factor.

3-4. Describe the methods for meeting status needs to motivate employees.

3-5. Describe the key factor to effective delegation.

3-6. Contrast integrative bargaining with distributive bargaining for conflict resolution.

Application Question

3-7. Teresa is a team leader for a group of fifteen customer service representatives (CSRs) in a medium-sized agency. Recently, there have been problems with disagreements between individuals within this group of CSRs. Teresa has had to intervene on several occasions and has met with several of the employees to discuss and resolve these issues.

   a. Explain how Teresa could emphasize superordinate goals as a strategy to deal with the conflict in her department.

   b. Explain how Teresa could use recognition to motivate the CSRs.

Educational Objective 4

Describe these specific aspects of the controlling function of management:

- The four steps in the control process
- The factors managers should consider when evaluating employee performance

---

Review Questions

4-1. Identify the four steps in the control process.

4-2. Explain how reporting systems are used in the control process.

4-3. Describe the purpose of control reports.

4-4. List the two areas in which managers can evaluate organizational and individual employee results.

4-5. Explain how a manager can implement corrective action when performance standards are not met.

4-6. Describe the development opportunities that could be included in an employee's performance plan.

4-7. Describe the sources of feedback for employee performance evaluations.

Answers to Assignment 2 Questions

NOTE: These answers are provided to give students a basic understanding of acceptable types of responses. They often are not the only valid answers and are not intended to provide an exhaustive response to the questions.

Educational Objective 1

1-1. The four functions of management are planning, organizing, leading, and controlling.

1-2. An effective and efficient organizational plan must have these four characteristics:

- *Unity*—Only one centralized guiding plan should be put into operation at a time to achieve the organization's mission and goals. Putting multiple plans into operation may cause confusion and can be counter to the mission and goals.

- *Continuity*—The organization's manager can build on previous plans and continually modify current plans (corporate, business, and functional) so they fit into a single organizational framework.

- *Accuracy*—Managers should gather and use all available relevant information in the planning process, recognizing that inaccuracy can result from incompleteness.

- *Flexibility*— Managers should be able to modify the plan when changes are necessary. Unless it is flexible, the plan cannot respond to the dynamic requirements of a changing environment.

1-3. Corporate plans are strategic, setting the overall course and direction for the organization. Strategic goals are long term, usually taking two to four years to accomplish. The organizational goals and corporate-level strategy should support the corporate mission. Generally, the corporate mission is a broad, concise statement of the primary corporate purpose, products, services, and markets, and it is designed to be long-standing.

1-4. A mission statement is broadly stated and needs based, meaning that it is focused on the desire to meet the needs of current and potential customers. A vision statement is intended to be an inspiring and positive description of what the organization aspires to become; it usually includes the values that guide the organization.

1-5. Budgets enable management to assign numbers to the goals for the planning period and create a means of measuring progress toward those goals. A budget must be written and realistic, and it must include senior management's vision and line managers' operating expertise.

1-6. Capital budgeting is the process of planning expenditures on assets whose returns are expected to extend beyond one year. Office renovations and the purchase of furnishings are examples of capital expenditures. Capital budgeting also includes long-term investment of excess cash. Organizations that have the excess cash required for such investments must evaluate the long-term risks as well as the returns on those investments.

1-7. Policies are guidelines for making decisions and performing activities. They may be stated narrowly or broadly. Procedures are an established series of steps or instructions for performing normal and recurring activities.

Educational Objective 2

2-1. Under a line organizational structure, the principal (agency owner) assigns tasks directly to the office personnel and is ultimately responsible for what the office personnel do.

2-2. The advantage of a line organization is simplicity. This structure clearly indicates to employees who their managers are and who has organizational responsibility. A line organization structure can also help managers respond quickly to customer service issues. Line organizations are efficient for small businesses.

2-3. The greatest disadvantage of a line organization is the possibility that the owner will be unable or unwilling to stop being involved in activities that are better performed by others. Often, when the business and the owner mature together, the owner has difficulty sharing authority.

2-4. The greatest advantage of functional organizations is that they are built around experts in each field. With specialized training in particular areas, these experts are better equipped to solve the problems in their functional areas than are line executives.

2-5. The line and staff organizational structure presents a few disadvantages. At times, staff people attempt to assume line authority because they want to see their ideas implemented. Conversely, because line people can override the ideas of the staff, ideas that improve effectiveness and efficiency may not be implemented. Also, a line and staff organizational structure may not be possible for small organizations simply because they have an insufficient number of employees.

2-6. A position description indicates where the position falls within the organization's hierarchy and the overall responsibilities for that description. Also, the specific job responsibilities and the nature and scope of the position.

2-7. Adequate staffing is important to an organization because its ability to meet short-term and long-term goals and objectives is largely based on having the right people in place at the right time to implement plans. Adequate staffing is also important in preparing for future growth, adapting to change, and sustaining employee morale.

2-8. Prospecting for employees in anticipation of future needs provides the organization with several benefits:

- It increases the odds of selecting the right person by developing a pool of potential candidates.

- It saves administrative time, effort, and expense when a position becomes available.

- It helps the organization achieve a competitive edge in the face of a shrinking labor supply.

2-9. Employers can identify prospects for employment by using various methods, including referrals; academic placement offices; employment agencies; and newspaper, magazine, or Internet advertisements.

2-10. The candidate evaluation process consists of these seven tasks:

- Contacting candidates
- Reviewing the job application
- Interviewing candidates
- Testing candidates
- Checking references
- Verifying candidates' experience and education
- Offering employment

2-11. The offer may take the form of a detailed employment contract, or it may simply be a letter outlining the offer.

Educational Objective 3

3-1. These are the three major aspects of leadership that are most important in an insurance agency environment:

- Motivating
- Delegating
- Managing conflict

3-2. If employees do not perceive that their needs can be satisfied, they have no incentive to act.

3-3. Wages should adequately reflect the difficulty and market value of a job. Money can be a destructive, negative factor if the salary level is perceived to be unfair relative to that provided by other organizations or relative to that provided to other employees in the same organization with similar responsibilities.

3-4. An assigned office, cubicle, or parking space; a certain title; or a territory of operations can provide such status.

3-5. The key to effective delegation is for managers to lead by communicating clearly and concisely when delegating a task. The manager must state expected results and clearly define the scope of the authority and responsibility.

3-6. Integrative bargaining is a form of cooperative negotiation in which the parties in conflict work together to achieve a mutually satisfactory resolution. In contrast, an example of distributive negotiation is as an employee negotiating for a raise from an employer who has had a financially difficult year.

3-7. These answers apply to the facts of Teresa's department.

a. Teresa could focus on the goals of the organization, such as sales targets, quality customer service, and queue waiting times and seek agreement on these to achieve greater organizational purpose. Keeping superordinate goals paramount helps the employees to remember that they are part of a larger organization with a shared mission that must be fulfilled, despite any differences within their department.

b. Recognition creates an atmosphere that reinforces and rewards outcomes that benefit the organization. The CSRs may be motivated to resolve differences and exhibit positive behaviors when a recognition system is in place. Positive reinforcement and recognition of individual accomplishments can be effective incentive. Such recognition could include employee of the month, personal thank you, or an announcement recognizing an employee's achievement.

Educational Objective 4

4-1. The control process consists of four steps:

- Establishing performance standards against which performance is to be evaluated

- Measuring results

- Comparing results against chosen performance standards

- Evaluating the results and implementing corrective action if the performance standards are not being met

4-2. Reporting systems gather and present information in a format useful for measuring results. These systems should be simple and should allow for easy comparison of results. Reports that are excessively time-consuming to prepare may not be valuable in the long run because of their adverse effect on employee or manager productivity. Reports should always be in writing.

4-3. Control reports are meant to present a comparison of performance against an established standard and to reveal improvement or decline. They should contain only key comparisons, measuring an employee's efficiency, quality of work, and responsiveness to customers in operational areas.

4-4. Managers can evaluate organizational and individual employee results in two areas: outputs and activities.

4-5. The reason for not meeting standards dictates what corrective actions should be taken. For example, failing to meet a sales standard may result from internal issues such as insufficient training or number of calls on qualified prospects. To correct these problems, the manager may require additional training or establish specific goals and criteria for improvement.

4-6. An employee's performance plan should include opportunities for development, such as training programs or participation in special projects, work teams, or task forces.

4-7. Performance feedback may be based solely on the manager's appraisal or may include input from co-workers or subordinates within the same department. Evaluations may also be solicited from insurers or customers outside of the organization, or co-workers in other departments within the organization who frequently interact with the employee.

Agency Sales Management

Educational Objectives

After learning the content of this assignment, you should be able to:

1. Describe the purposes of agency sales management.

2. Describe top-down and bottom-up agency sales management systems.

3. Describe the steps in the sales management process.

4. Describe the three steps involved in establishing a sales management organizational structure.

5. Explain why an agency plans for the following in order to meet its strategic goals:

   - Staffing the agency

   - Hiring new producers

   - Developing new and existing producers

6. Explain how an agency uses the following aspects of sales management operations in order to meet its strategic goals:

   - Producer compensation systems

   - Producer performance and accountability

7. Given a scenario regarding an agency sales manager meeting with the agency's producers, determine how both planning and operational elements discussed in the meeting contribute towards the agency's overall strategic goals.

Outline

▶ **Agencies and Sales Management**

    A. Maximize Production Efforts

    B. Promote Effectiveness and Efficiency

▶ **Sales Management Systems**

    A. Top-Down Systems

    B. Bottom-Up Systems

▶ **Agency Sales Management Planning—Developing a Process**

    A. Develop a Mission Statement

    B. Develop Goals

    C. Develop Strategies

    D. Develop Objectives

    E. Develop Budgets

    F. Establish Policies and Procedures

    G. Evaluate Results

▶ **Sales Management Organizational Structure**

    A. Types of Agency Sales Structures

    B. Define and Assign Responsibilities

    C. Group Responsibilities by Position

    D. Determine Job Interrelationships

▶ **Agency Sales Management Operations—Staffing and Producer Hiring**

    A. Staffing the Agency

    B. Hiring Producers

    C. Developing New and Existing Producers

▶ **Agency Sales Management Operations—Producer Compensation and Performance**

    A. Compensation Systems

    B. Setting Performance Standards

    C. Measuring Performance Results

    D. Using Reporting and Accountability Systems

    E. Conducting Performance Evaluations

    F. Taking Corrective Action

    G. Rewarding Employees

▶ **Agency Sales Management Case Study**

    A. Case Facts

    B. Case Analysis Tools

    C. Overview of Steps

    D. Introduction of the Agency's Overall Goals

    E. Presentation of the New Carrier Relationship

    F. Discussion of Sales Objectives

    G. Discussion of the Agency's Organizational Structure

    H. Presentation of New Mobile Technology

    I. Producer Development Opportunities

s.m.a.r.t.® tips   Use the SMART Online Practice Exams to test your understanding of the course material. You can review questions over a single assignment or multiple assignments, or you can take an exam over the entire course.

▶▶

For each assignment, you should define or describe each of the Key Words and Phrases and answer each of the Review and Application Questions.

Educational Objective 1
Describe the purposes of agency sales management.

Review Questions

1-1.   What is the primary purpose of agency sales management?

1-2.   What is a disadvantage of promoting an agency's best producer to the position of sales manager?

1-3.   What type of evaluation should an agency's principals perform before promoting a producer to a sales manager position?

1-4. Explain why agency sales management must be effective.

1-5. What are the results of efficient sales management?

1-6. List the typical features of IT systems that are available to provide more effective sales management for an agency.

Application Question

1-7. An insurance agency is growing, and the agency's principals are discussing how to most effectively manage the sales function. The agency is considering promoting one of the top producers to a sales manager position. However, their cost benefit analysis indicates this would result in a loss of approximately $40,000 per year in commissions. They do not want to hire a sales manager from outside the agency for various reasons. What is another alternative they could consider?

Educational Objective 2
Describe top-down and bottom-up agency sales management systems.

Key Words and Phrases

Top-down system

Bottom-up system

Review Questions

2-1. What two key factors are involved in the success of a sales management system?

2-2. Describe a top-down system for sales management.

2-3. What types of computer reports are useful to an agency with a top-down sales management system?

2-4. Describe a bottom-up system for sales management.

2-5. How would the information flow in a large agency with a bottom-up sales management system?

2-6. Describe how an agency's IT system can contribute to the success of a bottom-up system for sales management.

Application Question

2-7. A growing insurance agency is planning to purchase a new computer system. Explain why the agency's top-down or bottom-up sales management system should be an important factor in the purchasing decision.

Educational Objective 3
Describe the steps in the sales management process.

Review Questions

3-1. Describe the purpose of an agency's mission statement.

3-2. Describe the SMART method for developing sales goals.

3-3. Compare premium volume, business mix, and specialization sales strategies.

3-4. Identify what resource, in addition to money, should be addressed in sales management budgets.

3-5. Describe what typically results from not having written sales procedures.

3-6. Explain how an agency sales manager monitors the effectiveness of the agency's sales plan.

Application Question

3-7. A growing insurance agency has hired a sales manager. During the previous year, the agency's retention rate slipped below its historic 98 percent to 94 percent. The sales manager observes that producers are prospecting for new business, which results in growth, but not making frequent calls on existing customers. The manager also observes that many clerical functions the CSRs previously performed are now automated by a new computer system. Additionally, there is no written manual of sales procedures. The agency's principals have set a goal of a 20 percent increase in commissions, with 98 percent retention. The strategy is premium volume growth. What are some sales planning steps the sales manager should take?

Educational Objective 4

Describe the three steps involved in establishing a sales management organizational structure.

Review Questions

4-1. What are the three steps in establishing an organizational structure for an insurance agency's sales function?

4-2.   What are the major activities associated with the sales function in a property-casualty insurance agency?

4-3.   What is the purpose of all of the responsibilities performed in an insurance agency?

4-4.   How should management examine an existing agency's organizational structure?

4-5.   How does the grouping of responsibilities into positions help an agency achieve an effective sales organizational structure?

4-6. What do agency employees need to understand about interrelationships among jobs in the agency?

Application Question

4-7. A new sales manager at an insurance agency is evaluating the existing organizational structure. In the present structure, the producers are completely responsible for all eight of the key production accountabilities. The producers are very busy, and the agency is growing. The support staff is not as busy as the producers because of a new computer system that has automated many functions, such as submitting applications to underwriters. How might the new sales manager redesign the organizational structure?

Educational Objective 5

Explain why an agency plans for the following in order to meet its strategic goals:

- **Staffing the agency**
- **Hiring new producers**
- **Developing new and existing producers**

Review Questions

5-1. Describe the four major types of staff in an insurance agency.

5-2. Explain the role of the ratio of producers to support staff in determining an agency's effectiveness in reaching sales goals.

5-3. Explain how often agencies should plan staffing levels.

5-4. Describe the two major reasons for hiring a producer at an agency.

5-5. List the four major types of educational and training methods available for producers and other agency staff.

5-6. Explain why producer development must go beyond merely satisfying licensing requirements.

Application Question

5-7. A growing insurance agency recently hired a full-time sales manager and invested in a new information technology (IT) system. Explain whether the agency should reevaluate its ratio of producers to support staff at this time.

Educational Objective 6

Explain how an agency uses the following aspects of sales management operations in order to meet its strategic goals:

- **Producer compensation systems**
- **Producer performance and accountability**

Review Questions

6-1.   What are the three most commonly used producer compensation systems?

6-2.   Which type of producer typically benefits most from the commission-only system of producer compensation?

6-3.   List three types of performance standards for evaluating agency job performance.

6-4. How are agency job performance results measured?

6-5. When is corrective action needed on an agency-wide performance basis and on an individual performance basis?

6-6. What two important results can be accomplished by recognition of top producers?

Application Question

6-7. An agency's sales manager has determined that the agency's top producers make an average of three calls on prospects and two calls on existing customers each day. The sales manager is thinking of using this as a performance standard for all of the agency's producers. Explain the type of standard this would represent and how the sales manager would measure performance.

Educational Objective 7

Given a scenario regarding an agency sales manager meeting with the agency's producers, determine how both planning and operational elements discussed in the meeting contribute towards the agency's overall strategic goals.

Application Question

7-1. Allen is the new sales manager at an insurance agency. The agency's principals want to achieve 10 percent growth in commissions this year. Allen and the principals agree that they are going to use a bottom-up approach to sales planning, supported by their new computer system. Allen schedules a meeting with all of the agency's producers.

   a. Two producers live and work out of state. Should Allen require them to attend the meeting in person? Explain.

   b. In a bottom-up approach to sales planning, who would set individual producers' sales goals?

   c. Allen discusses the new mobile technology. How can this technology assist the producers in meeting their sales goals?

Answers to Assignment 3 Questions

NOTE: These answers are provided to give students a basic understanding of acceptable types of responses. They often are not the only valid answers and are not intended to provide an exhaustive response to the questions.

Educational Objective 1

1-1. The primary purpose of agency sales management is to maximize production efforts.

1-2. The result is often a decrease in sales by the producer after the promotion.

1-3. The agency's principals should perform a cost/benefit analysis that evaluates the producer's sales commissions versus the cost of hiring a new agency sales manager.

1-4. Agency sales management must be effective because success in selling insurance products and providing service is crucial to the agency's ongoing success.

1-5. Efficient sales management helps reduce or eliminate wasted time and expense resulting from duplication of effort, inadequate staffing or training, and misdirected resources.

1-6. These are typical features of such systems:

- Client information and customer service applications

- Interface with insurer systems

- Commission calculation and tracking

- Agency sales goals and performance

- Individual producer sales goals and performance

1-7. The agency's principals could consider purchasing or upgrading an IT system to provide resources for more effective and efficient sales management. Such a system could provide reports on producers' sales efforts and results as well as assisting producers to interface with insurers and following up on key customer activities.

Educational Objective 2

2-1. A management system can result in successful sales if there is IT system support and consensus on goals between producers and management.

2-2. Some agencies use a top-down system for sales management. Producers are given specific goals to help the agency reach its overall goals. In large organizations, the goals work their way down through several levels.

2-3. The types of reports should include tracking of agency and producer sales results against goals to monitor producers and branch offices to ensure they are on target for achieving their goals.

2-4. Some agencies manage sales with a bottom-up system, which involves producers and branch managers in larger agencies in setting both individual and agency sales goals.

2-5. In larger agencies, the information flows from small agency units through large agency units and from producers to production departments through multiple offices.

2-6. The IT systems used by agencies with a bottom-up focus must be able to provide the data and reports to support this type of sales management. Various systems are available for insurance agencies that provide real-time information on the agency's sales performance as well as market information.

2-7. The IT system the agency uses must support the type of sales management system the agency uses. In a top-down system, managers must have access to computer reports to monitor producers' progress against their assigned goals in order to meet sales goals. In a bottom-up sales management system, producers should have real-time access to production reports and market information to set and achieve their goals.

Educational Objective 3

3-1. An agency's mission statement is a broad statement of the agency's purpose and overarching goals. The mission statement frames a vision for the agency and its producers.

3-2. The SMART method uses specific, measurable, achievable, relevant, and time-bound criteria to develop sales goals.

3-3. Premium volume strategies are designed to increase the agency's volume to a planned level. Business mix strategies involve a plan to change the mix of agency business. Specialization strategies include growth in narrowly defined areas or in a predetermined market.

3-4. Although the most common aspect of budgeting is to allocate money in a way that best serves the agency's goals, the allocation of people and time is also an important aspect of budgeting. Just as the agency sales manager allocates available funds, the sales manager should allocate the producers' and CSRs' time.

3-5. Pressures of daily work can often take precedence over creating procedures. The result of this focus can be duplication of effort and inefficient processing, which affect both sales and servicing.

3-6. The agency sales manager monitors the agency's sales plan by examining individual weekly and monthly production reports, conducting sales meetings, and determining how results compare with the plan's goals.

3-7. The sales manager should work with the producers to set specific objectives for commissions and customer retention. Additionally, the sales manager should develop a budget for the sales staff resources and consider allocating CSR resources to prospecting so that producers can spend additional time meeting with current clients. Finally, the sales manager should develop written sales procedures.

Educational Objective 4

4-1. Establishing an organizational structure involves three distinct steps:

- Define and assign responsibilities

- Group responsibilities by position

- Determine job interrelationships

4-2. For an agency producing property-casualty insurance, these activities can include sales management, property-casualty sales, new and renewal business placement with insurers, policy rating and quoting, other customer service support of the sales process, accounting services and support, IT support of the overall sales process (including marketing support and accountability tools), and administrative services.

4-3. Insurance agencies are sales organizations, and all responsibilities performed in the organization ultimately support the producer and the sales function.

4-4. When examining an existing agency's organizational structure, management must disregard the current structure and list the responsibilities performed, regardless of existing positions or individuals handling those responsibilities.

4-5. After defining and assigning responsibilities, the agency must group them by position. Grouping responsibilities into positions maximizes the agency's use of the human and economic resources that support the sales management organization.

4-6. Agency management should communicate the interrelationships among jobs in the agency to their employees. Agency employees should understand how their jobs relate, how they fit into the agency sales management organizational structure, and to whom they report.

4-7. The new sales manager might organize the sales staff into teams and assign some production responsibilities to support staff. Having support staff assist with prospecting and customer service would help the producers and also help CSRs develop the skill and knowledge to perhaps eventually become producers.

Educational Objective 5

5-1. There are four major types of staff in an insurance agency:

- Managers are responsible for meeting the overall goals of the agency. Sales managers are responsible for meeting the agency's sales goals—specifically, answering to the agency owner or principal(s).

- Producers are licensed to sell insurance products and are key to an agency's success in meeting sales objectives.

- Customer service representatives (CSRs) are also licensed and have extensive responsibility in providing service to customers and assisting producers with sales functions.

- Administrative and support staff perform functions that assist managers and key staff members in meeting the agency's goals.

5-2. The sales manager, along with the agency's other managers, must plan the ratio of producers to CSRs and support staff, and the staffing level required for each type of position. A ratio with a high number of producers to a small number of support staff may result in producers inefficiently spending time on administrative functions. A ratio with a small number of producers to a high level of support staff may result in insufficient resources devoted to selling. To have maximum effectiveness and efficiency to reach sales goals, the ratio of producers to other staff must be the right one for each agency. An agency's managers should plan for current and anticipated business needs in determining staffing ratios.

5-3. Agencies should plan their staffing levels on at least an annual basis. As agencies grow and technology continues to change, the management structure as well as the ratio of producers to support staff may need to change to provide optimal effectiveness.

5-4. The two major reasons for hiring a producer at an agency are to replace a producer who has left the agency and to increase sales for the agency.

5-5. The four major types of educational and training methods available for producers and other agency staff involve educational organizations, training and continuing education, producer associations, and insurers.

5-6. Producer development must go beyond merely satisfying licensing requirements. Insurance is both complex and dynamic, so producers need to have current knowledge and skills. Also important for both the individual producer and the agency is that producers are fully engaged in their profession. Continual professional development can help ensure this engagement.

5-7. Yes, the agency should reevaluate its producer to support staff ratio shortly after making the major changes of hiring a full-time sales manager and upgrading the IT system. Functions that were formerly performed by administrative staff may now be automated, and customer service representatives who used to perform clerical functions may be able to assume production responsibilities because of efficiencies gained from the new computer system.

Educational Objective 6

6-1. The three most commonly used producer compensation systems are (1) commission only, (2) salary only, and (3) salary and commission.

6-2. Generally, the commission-only system works well with experienced producers who have an established book of business.

6-3. These are types of performance standards:

- Budgetary
- Sales
- Engineered
- Individual performance
- Judgment and experience
- Historical

6-4. Results are measured by comparing the performance standards to actual results. Most agencies measure both overall agency results and individual employee results.

6-5. Agency-wide action is required when overall agency goals have not been achieved. Corrective action may involve changes in agency goals, systems, and/or staff. On an individual basis, corrective action is required when an employee is not performing up to the established standards. Such action may involve training, a change in responsibilities, and/or probation or dismissal.

6-6. Recognition rewards successful producers and can also motivate other producers.

6-7. The sales manager would develop an engineered standard. The standard could be three prospecting calls and two existing customer calls each day for all producers. Producers would be measured according to whether they met, exceeded, or failed to meet the engineered standard.

Educational Objective 7

7-1. These answers relate to Allen's sales planning meeting.

    a.   Although Allen could invite them to attend in person if this is feasible, they could participate via a Web-based meeting program or conference call.

    b.   In a bottom-up approach to sales planning, the individual producers would be involved in setting their sales goals to match the overall agency goals.

    c.   The new technology can offer improved communications for producers, who are frequently out of the office on sales calls. This technology can provide data, quotations, and tracking of performance against goals for producers to use while they are traveling to meet with clients.

Personal Production Plans

Educational Objectives

After learning the content of this assignment, you should be able to:

1. Explain how the various steps in the personal production planning process enable a producer to achieve specific goals that are consistent with the agency's overall strategic objectives.

2. Explain how a personal production plan supports the agency's strategic goals and how an agency uses a personal production plans summary.

3. Describe five strategies producers use to manage time effectively.

4. Describe the negotiating rules and techniques that are important in principled negotiating and how they can result in a "win-win" scenario.

5. Given a scenario regarding an insurance agency, demonstrate how a producer, using a well-designed personal production plan and good time management, is able to negotiate a "win-win" resolution on an account.

Outline

▶ **Personal Production Plan Process**
- A. Develop a Mission Statement
- B. Develop Goals
- C. Develop Strategies
- D. Develop Objectives
- E. Develop Budgets
- F. Establish Policies and Procedures
- G. Monitor the Plan

▶ **Personal Production Plans Summary**

▶ **Time Management**
- A. Eliminate Time-Wasters
- B. Set Priorities
- C. Prepare for Meetings
- D. Plan
- E. Manage Phone Calls and E-Mail

▶ **Negotiation**
- A. Know the Other Party
- B. Avoid "Single-Issue" Negotiation
- C. Do Not Push the Advantage
- D. Deliver More Than Promised

▶ **Personal Production Plan Case Study**
- A. Case Facts
- B. Case Analysis Tools
- C. Overview of Steps
  1. Devise a Personal Production Plan
  2. Use Time Management Techniques
  3. Apply Negotiation Skills

s.m.a.r.t. tips   The SMART Online Practice Exams can be tailored to cover specific assignments, so you can focus your studies on topics you want to master.

▶▶

For each assignment, you should define or describe each of the Key Words and Phrases and answer each of the Review and Application Questions.

Educational Objective 1

Explain how the various steps in the personal production planning process enable a producer to achieve specific goals that are consistent with the agency's overall strategic objectives.

Key Word or Phrase

Personal production plan

Review Questions

1-1. List the seven steps used to develop a personal production plan.

1-2. Identify the ideal characteristics of a personal goal.

1-3. Identify the ideal characteristics of a strategy.

1-4. Define objectives.

1-5. Contrast policies with procedures.

1-6. Identify examples of approaches agencies take to monitoring plans.

Educational Objective 2

Explain how a personal production plan supports the agency's strategic goals and how an agency uses a personal production plans summary.

Review Questions

2-1. Identify the purpose of an agency production plans summary.

▶▶

2-2. Identify the elements that support a producer's annual production goal.

2-3. Explain how a model personal production plan gives a producer a set of self-directed sales activities.

2-4. Identify why an agency that negotiates a personal production plan and assists the producer with meeting goals and objectives helps the producer generate new business more rapidly.

Educational Objective 3
Describe five strategies producers use to manage time effectively.

Review Questions

3-1. List five time management strategies producers can use to increase the time available for selling.

3-2. Identify the time-related benefit that a producer may incur by establishing and adhering to a sales system with a personal production plan.

3-3. List three methods for eliminating the "management by crisis" time-waster.

3-4. List three methods for eliminating personal disorganization.

3-5. List two methods for eliminating procrastination.

3-6. Contrast an important task with an urgent task.

Educational Objective 4

Describe the negotiating rules and techniques that are important in principled negotiating and how they can result in a "win-win" scenario.

Review Questions

4-1. Identify the two determinations that constitute knowing the other party in a negotiation.

4-2. Explain why knowing the prospect's style of doing business is essential to effective negotiating for producers.

4-3. Identify the likely result of a "single-issue" negotiation.

4-4. Identify the benefit of giving something more than promised after negotiations.

Educational Objective 5

Given a scenario regarding an insurance agency, demonstrate how a producer, using a well-designed personal production plan and good time management, is able to negotiate a "win-win" resolution on an account.

Application Question

5-1. Rasheda is a newly hired producer whose personal mission statement is "To provide premier risk management services to my community." This aspiration correlates with her agency's goal of increasing its personal lines business during the calendar year. Rasheda recognizes that to fulfill her personal mission statement, she needs to increase her risk management acumen by taking continuing education classes.

  a. Rasheda examines her personal mission statement and settles on "I will take risk management courses" as one of her goals. Explain whether this has the characteristics of an ideal goal.

b. Rasheda negotiates a goal with her manager that requires her to take and pass two risk management course examinations during the calendar year. Rasheda decides to focus on taking and passing four risk management course examinations during the calendar year. Identify the negotiating technique exemplified by Rasheda's focus.

c. By July of the calendar year during which Rasheda wishes to achieve her education goal, she still has not signed up for any risk management courses. She often finds herself on the verge of enrolling, only to be lured away by simpler or more immediately satisfying office tasks. Identify the time waster that appears to impede Rasheda's progress and list ways she can combat it.

Answers to Assignment 4 Questions

NOTE: These answers are provided to give students a basic understanding of acceptable types of responses. They often are not the only valid answers and are not intended to provide an exhaustive response to the questions.

Educational Objective 1

1-1. These are the seven steps used to develop a personal production plan:

  a. Develop a mission statement

  b. Develop goals

  c. Develop strategies

  d. Develop objectives

  e. Determine budgets

  f. Establish policies and procedures

  g. Monitor the plan

1-2. Like agency goals, personal goals should be specific, measurable, achievable, relevant, and time bound (SMART).

1-3. An ideal strategy is personal, relates to the organization's mission and goals, and narrows the focus of personal activities while remaining broad enough to allow a variety of sales activities.

1-4. Objectives are milestones toward goals and should be directed at accomplishing the goals they support.

1-5. Whereas policies indicate what should be done, procedures indicate how things should be done.

1-6. Examples of approaches agencies take to monitoring plans include self-monitoring by producers and monitoring by the agency principal or sales manager at weekly, monthly, or quarterly sales meetings.

Educational Objective 2

2-1. An agency production plans summary provides an overview of all of the producers' goals, which should support the agency's goals and mission.

2-2. A producer's annual production goal is supported by underlying annual objectives and key production activities, which are monitored monthly.

2-3. A model personal production plan gives a producer a set of self-directed sales activities that are derived from and support the goals and objectives. Independent, entrepreneurial activities encourage the producer to focus on executing the production plan.

2-4. An agency that negotiates a personal production plan and assists the producer with meeting goals and objectives helps the producer generate new business more rapidly because the producer may take less time than otherwise to become productive, contributing to the agency's profits more quickly and reducing the time and money invested in the producer.

Educational Objective 3

3-1. These are five time management strategies producers can use to increase the time available for selling:

- Eliminate time-wasters

- Set priorities

- Prepare for meetings

- Plan

- Manage phone calls and e-mails

3-2. Producers who establish and adhere to a sales system with a personal production plan can mitigate the effects of many time-wasters.

3-3. These are three methods for eliminating the "management by crisis" time-waster:

- Set and adhere to deadlines to avoid self-created crises.

- Build extra time into schedules to handle unanticipated events.

- Conduct an after-action review after each crisis to determine how to avoid or better manage future crises.

3-4. These are three methods for eliminating personal disorganization:

- Group similar tasks and perform them at the same time.

- Take advantage of the agency management system software's organizational tools.

- Work on tasks for one project at a time.

3-5. These are two methods for eliminating procrastination:

- Select the top two or three tasks daily from your "To Do" list that are important and urgent. Complete these tasks first to avoid being distracted by them throughout the day.

- Complete the hardest task(s) for the day first.

3-6. An important task can be defined as any task that leads to accomplishing goals. An urgent task is one that demands immediate action.

Educational Objective 4

4-1. Knowing the other party requires determining the other person's style of doing business and the other person's goals.

4-2. Knowing the prospect's style of doing business is essential to effective negotiating because it helps the producer determine how to negotiate.

4-3. The likely result of a "single-issue" negotiation is a "win-lose" scenario.

4-4. Giving something more than promised after negotiations are complete creates an important advantage in future negotiations with the same customer.

Educational Objective 5

5-1. These answers are based on producer Rasheda's case facts:

    a. Rasheda's goal, "I will take risk management courses," lacks four of the five required character-istics of an ideal goal. It is not specific. The goal is also not measurable. The goal is not time-bound. The goal is relevant because it correlates with her personal mission statement. Because the goal is not specific, measurable, or time-bound, it cannot be considered achievable.

    b. The negotiating technique exemplified by Rasheda's focus on taking and passing four risk management examinations as opposed to two is delivering more than is promised.

    c. The time waster that appears to impede Rasheda's progress is procrastination. These are ways she can combat it:

        • Select the top two or three tasks daily from her "To Do" list that are important and urgent and complete them first.

        • Complete the hardest task(s) for the day first.

Exam Information

About Institutes Exams

Exam questions are based on the Educational Objectives stated in the course guide and textbook. The exam is designed to measure whether you have met those Educational Objectives. The exam does not necessarily test every Educational Objective. It tests over a balanced sample of Educational Objectives.

How to Prepare for Institutes Exams

What can you do to prepare for an Institutes exam? Students who pass Institutes exams do the following:

▶ Use the assigned study materials. Focus your study on the Educational Objectives presented at the beginning of each course guide assignment. Thoroughly read the textbook and any other assigned materials, and then complete the course guide exercises. Choose a study method that best suits your needs; for example, participate in a traditional class, online class, or informal study group; or study on your own. Use The Institutes' SMART Study Aids (if available) for practice and review. If this course has an associated SMART Online Practice Exams product, you will find an access code on the inside back cover of this course guide. This access code allows you to print a full practice exam and to take additional online practice exams that will simulate an actual credentialing exam.

▶ Become familiar with the types of test questions asked on the exam. The practice exam in this course guide or in the SMART Online Practice Exams product will help you understand the different types of questions you will encounter on the exam.

▶ Maximize your test-taking time. Successful students use the sample exam in the course guide or in the SMART Online Practice Exams product to practice pacing themselves. Learning how to manage your time during the exam ensures that you will complete all of the test questions in the time allotted.

Types of Exam Questions

The exam for this course consists of objective questions of several types.

The Correct-Answer Type

In this type of question, the question stem is followed by four responses, one of which is absolutely correct. Select the *correct* answer.

Which one of the following persons evaluates requests for insurance to determine which applicants are accepted and which are rejected?

a.   The premium auditor

b.   The loss control representative

c.   The underwriter

d.   The risk manager

The Best-Answer Type

In this type of question, the question stem is followed by four responses, only one of which is best, given the statement made or facts provided in the stem. Select the *best* answer.

Several people within an insurer might be involved in determining whether an applicant for insurance is accepted. Which one of the following positions is primarily responsible for determining whether an applicant for insurance is accepted?

a.   The loss control representative

b.   The customer service representative

c.   The underwriter

d.   The premium auditor

The Incomplete-Statement or Sentence-Completion Type

In this type of question, the last part of the question stem consists of a portion of a statement rather than a direct question. Select the phrase that *correctly* or *best* completes the sentence.

> Residual market plans designed for individuals who are unable to obtain insurance on their personal property in the voluntary market are called
>
> a.   VIN plans.
>
> b.   Self-insured retention plans.
>
> c.   Premium discount plans.
>
> d.   FAIR plans.

"All of the Above" Type

In this type of question, only one of the first three answers could be correct, or all three might be correct, in which case the best answer would be "All of the above." Read all the answers and select the *best* answer.

> When a large commercial insured's policy is up for renewal, who is likely to provide input to the renewal decision process?
>
> a.   The underwriter
>
> b.   The loss control representative
>
> c.   The producer
>
> d.   All of the above

"All of the following, EXCEPT:" Type

In this type of question, responses include three correct answers and one answer that is incorrect or is clearly the least correct. Select the *incorrect* or *least correct* answer.

> All of the following adjust insurance claims, EXCEPT:
>
> a.   Insurer claims representatives
>
> b.   Premium auditors
>
> c.   Producers
>
> d.   Independent adjusters

Index

Page numbers in boldface refer to pages where the word or phrase is defined.